A MOTHER IN HISTORY

A
Mother
in History

BY JEAN STAFFORD

FARRAR, STRAUS AND GIROUX

NEW YORK

Sections of this book appeared originally in *McCall's* magazine, and I would like to thank Miss Barbara Lawrence of its staff for her editorial acumen. I am grateful, too, for the contributions of Mr. Lon Tinkle, Mr. Hermes Nye, Mr. Hugh Aynesworth, Mrs. Arch Swank, and Mrs. John Satton.

J. S.

I

I

In a tidy, unexceptional little house, on an unexceptional block of similar houses (they were seedy, but they were not squalid, and in some of their front yards roses grew) in Fort Worth, Mrs. Marguerite Oswald received me one steamy May afternoon. Without preambulatory small talk, beyond asking me whether I found the air-conditioning cool or not cool enough (it was exactly right), she plunged straightaway into her memoirs—or rather, into those parts of her memoirs having to do with the arrest and murder of her son Lee Harvey Oswald that catapulted her to international renown. In the recitative of this, President Kennedy was little more than the deus ex machina, essential but never on stage.

3

Her voice had a considerable histrionic range; in a moment's time, she could shift her tone from resignation to irony, from sonorous patriotism to personal indignation, but at all times a central intelligence was at the controls, regulating the pitch and volume as she entered the successive roles of mother, citizen, widow, public figure. There was a suggestion of elocution lessons, nearly forgotton but learned well, long ago; and there was more than a suggestion of rehearsal and past performance— she spoke almost always in complete sentences, she was never visibly caught off guard.

She declared at the beginning that she was "not a mother defending her son," but was "speaking for history," since history, she is persuaded, has been deformed by the press and by the report of the Warren Commission's inquiry into President Kennedy's assassination, which is "all lies, lies, lies."

I had come to Texas to see Mrs. Oswald because she is, as she was frequently to tell me, "a mother in history," and while she remains peripheral to the immediate events of the Dallas killings, she is inherent to the evolution of the reasons for them. She is inherent, that is, if we accept (as I do) the premise that her son had something to do with the assassination and accept the further premise that the

child is father of the man : we need to know the in-
fluences and accidents and loves and antipathies and
idiosyncrasies that were the ingredients making up
the final compound. I hoped that Mrs. Oswald would
be able to tell me what these had been.

For all practical purposes, she was her son's only
parent, since his father died before he was born
and her later marriage lasted too short a time to
have much effect on him. Relatives are often (perhaps more often than not) the last people on earth
to know anything about each other. Still, there was
the possibility, and I had come down from Connecticut to explore it.

Mrs. Oswald, an inactive Lutheran, believes that
"if ye seek, ye shall find," that at last "truth will
prevail," and to correct the false impressions of her
son and herself under which most of the nation and
most of the world labor, she is dedicating her life
to her own investigation. From morning, when she
rises early, until night, she is at work "researching
the case," collating newspaper stories, studying
theories of conspiracy (right-wing, left-wing,
wingless, Catholic, Baptist, Jewish, Black Muslim,
anarchist, fascist, federalist, masterminded by the
cops, masterminded by the robbers) that have been
propounded from Los Angeles to West Berlin; read-

ing between the lines of the Warren Report and scrutinizing the errors of omission in it and those of commission, and the ambiguities and the garbles. She accepts any invitation anywhere to appear on platforms or on television screens to pass on her observations and to interpret them. For several months after the assassination, she was strenuously peripatetic, popping up all over in this country and in Canada. "My theme is the American way of life," she said to me, "and this, of course, is what I talked about."

"I want the truth known," she said, sitting upright on a sofa, her hands crossed at the wrists, palm upward. "I believe the American people are entitled to the truth and I believe they want to know. Now I will agree that immediately after the assassination, and while President Johnson was taking the place of President Kennedy, let me say in all respect that this was not the time to bring these truths before the public. But after his time in office most people think—I don't agree, but that's beside the point—that he is a very powerful President, and the assassination itself has subsided. I think these truths should be leaked now, and if in the leaking they can prove to me that my son was the assassin of President Kennedy, I won't commit suicide or drop dead. I will accept the facts as a good straight human being. But up until this day they have not shown me any proof and I have things in my possession to disprove many things they say. I understand all the testimony off the cuff is in Washington and will be locked up for seventy-five years. Well, I've got news for you. It will not be for seventy-five years, because if today or tomorrow I am dead or killed, what I have in my possession will be known. And I in my lifetime have got to continue what I have been doing, using my emotional stability and speaking out whenever I can. Would you like a cup of coffee?"

Because there was no hiatus between the proclamation of unwavering purpose and the hospitable, colloquial question, and because both were delivered in the same tone and at the same pace, I did not immediately take it in, but in a moment I did and said I would. (The drinking of coffee in Texas is almost as involuntary as respiration. One night I went into a restaurant in Dallas where, on every table, there was a glass pot of coffee kept bubbling over a candle-warmer. One or two of my guests poured out cups for themselves at once, following this aperitif with the Jack Daniel's and Johnnie Walker I had brought in a brown paper bag. I had forgotten, or had never known, that in Texas you produced your own liquor in public places and ordered setups just as in the oldentime.)

While Mrs. Oswald busied herself in the kitchen that abutted on the dinette at the end of the living room, she did not pause in her soliloquy. She asked herself questions and answered them in patient asides: "All the news mediums said he was such a failure in life. A failure in life?" she cried out in stunned disbelief. "He was twenty-four years old when he was murdered! The attorneys that are interviewing these witnesses make a hundred to a hundred and fifty dollars a day and they never lived this type life. Lee Harvey a failure? I am smiling. I think it took courage for a young boy to go to Russia at twenty, for whatever reason he went. I find this a very intelligent boy, and I think he's coming out in history as a very fine person."

Generally dropping the final "g's" of gerunds in a relaxed, rustic way, she spoke in the accent and the cadences of that part of New Orleans to which she was native, an accent that my late husband, A. J. Liebling, once described as "hard to distinguish from the accent of Hoboken, Jersey City, and Astoria, Long Island, where the Al Smith inflection, extinct in Manhattan, has taken refuge." "Point" becomes "pernt," and, conversely, "person" becomes "poyson."

Accustomed as she was to public speaking, Mrs. Oswald did not seem to be addressing me specifically but, rather, a large congregation; this was to be her manner with me on each of the three occasions I saw her. Taking advantage of my anonymity in this quiet crowd and of the fact that her back was turned, I looked around the room in the snoopy way women do when they are in other women's houses, and tried to think what sort of occupant I would assign to it if I did not already know who she was.

The house itself was a white stucco bungalow divided into two apartments, and as I had come up the short path, I had noticed a "For Rent" sign at the approach to the other side. Each apartment consisted of a living room—dining room that then turned a corner and became a kitchen; off the living room there was a small bedroom, and off that, a bath. The two kitchen doors debouched onto a common back porch, screened and looking out to a downward sloping lawn and pleasant shade trees.

The space was limited, but Mrs. Oswald had arranged her furniture adeptly, so that I did not feel nudged or threatened, and the furniture itself,

9

while it was middle-aged and had been nondescript all its life (except for a Danish modern chair upholstered in carroty polyethylene), was solid and in good repair and comfortable. The armchair I sat in was hard enough and soft enough, and there was an adequate table to the right of it on which stood an ashtray, a small vase of artificial violets, and a copy of *The Wounded Land*, Hans Habe's highstrung book on the American state of mind following the assassination. The walls were that general color that can be called beige or ecru or bone or buff or oatmeal, and hanging on the longest, over a sofa thronged with multiform and multicolored cushions, was a print of Whistler's "Mother." The glass that protected it was spotless and the brass identification plate was smartly burnished. I could not tell whether the picture was a recent acquisition or whether it was daily treated with polish and a chamois skin; clearly, it was cherished. On another wall, but oblique to my line of vision, there hung what seemed to be a copper scroll; I wanted to get up and look at it, but I felt this would be presumptuous, particularly because it was over a writing desk where orderly piles of papers were laid out to which my Paul Pry eye would be bound to stray. Near the television set (it confronted the sofa, and the vantage point from which Ben Casey would be observed was directly under Mrs. Whistler) there was a low tripod on which stood a jardiniere planted with crotons whose patterns were picked out in assertive shades of purple and red and leonine yellow; the health of these leaves was so obviously robust that they testified to a green thumb and made a puzzling contrast to the fake flowers and fake emperor grapes in other parts of the room. I had noticed the same phenomenon in the small front yard, where heather, far from home and made of wax and wire, emerged from a plastic pot toward which a few late tulips leaned their mortal, languid heads.

Mrs. Oswald, pouring hot water over instant coffee, was saying, "I can absolutely prove my son innocent. I can do it any time I want by going to Washington, D.C., with some pictures,[1] but I won't do it that way. I want to get my story before the public, so young and old all over the world will know the truth. Why don't I go to Washington?" With this question, she turned to face me, arms akimbo. Embattled, but at the same time an imperturbable strategist, she answered it: "Because they've been so ugly to me, to me and my boy. I'll

[1] See Appendix I, page 117.

1 1

write a book and the title of it will be *One and One Make Two* or *This and That*. Oh, I could write three books or five books! I could write books and *books* on what I know and what I have researched."

My own research, this cursory study of her living room, had yielded little more than the evidence that whoever lived here was a good housekeeper of modest means and a mild affection for bric-a-brac, so I gave up my elementary sleuthing and, hoping to set her back in time to the days before the concussion that had stunned the world, I asked her about her early life in New Orleans. But if she had any nostalgia for that most raffish and romantic and sweet and sinful city, she had suppressed it, and she brushed me aside as if there were no time for frivolous parentheses when the business at hand was history.

"Now maybe Lee Harvey Oswald was the assassin," she pursued, stirring the coffee. "But does that make him a louse? No, no! Killing does not necessarily mean badness. You find killing in some very fine homes for one reason or another. And as we all know, President Kennedy was a dying man. So I say it is possible that my son was chosen to shoot him in a mercy killing for the security of the country. And if this is true, it was a fine thing to do and my son is a hero."

"I had not heard that President Kennedy was dying," I said, staggered by this cluster of fictions stated as irrefutable fact. Some mercy killing! The methods used in this instance must surely be unique in the annals of euthanasia.

"Oh, yes," she went on with authority. My ignorance did not surprise her; she plainly was accustomed to dealing with people who, either through laziness or want of opportunity, did not know the ABC's of the case. "It's been in many articles that President Kennedy was a dying President, that he had Atkinson's disease, which is a disease of the kidney, and we know that he had three operations on his back and that he would have been a lingering President. For security reasons, we could not have a lingering President, because of our conflicts with other nations." She turned to me with her sociable smile and asked. "Do you take cream and sugar, sweetheart?"

Her affable face was round and lineless, and the skin that covered her small bones was delicate; her eyes were clear behind glasses in pale frames; and her clean white hair, only a little smudged with leftover gray, was pulled back straight into a plump and faultless bun. She wore a lime-green sheath that was appropriate to her short stature and her tubular, well-corseted construction. She would, I thought, be called "modish." Her general appearance and her demeanor were consistent with the several roles she has played in her fifty-eight years: insurance agent, saleslady, manageress of lingerie shops, switchboard operator, practical nurse. Terms of endearment came naturally to her lips, as they do to those of many Southern women; she could have been the stand-in and the off-stage voice for the woman from whom I had bought a rain cape in Neiman-Marcus that morning, who rejected the first one I tried on, saying, "No, honey, that just won't do. Your little dress shows." A Northerner is at first taken aback, then is seduced, then realizes —sometimes too late—that these blandishments are unconscious and wholly noncommittal and one need not feel obliged to reciprocate by buying the next rain cape. (In this case I did, and it comes nicely below the hems of all my little dresses.)

Mrs. Oswald, having delivered my creamed and sugared coffee, reestablished herself with her own cup on the sofa beneath her generic sister (fleetingly I wondered how Whistler, a noteworthy scrapper, had got along with Mrs. W.) and continued. "Now it could have been that my son and the Secret Service were all involved in a mercy killing. I have thought about this seriously. We teach our boys to kill in war and we don't think a thing about it, yet if these same boys kill someone on the street they are lawfully put in jail or else electrocuted, which is right. So why wouldn't it be just a normal thing to have a mercy killing of the President?"

She uttered the word "normal" without a suggestion of inverted commas, and I think this is exactly what she meant; as for "mercy killing," she made that sound as commonplace as the use of aspirin to bring down a fever.

"If he was dying of an incurable disease, this would be for the security of our country. Now when President Kennedy came to Fort Worth, Texas, for one night, there was an article in the paper that said the maid at the Hotel Texas had fixed his room for him and had to re-do the bed because he had his own hard mattress. Even for one night! He must have been a very bad man." (I was momentarily startled, but realized that this was merely a slip of the tongue.) "And his rocking chair is still the way it was, with the towel in the back because he was in such pain."

There floated across my mind a cloudy recollection of having heard (after the assassination, I thought) it rumored that the President had Addison's disease, which is not a distemper of the kidneys but a malfunction of the adrenal gland, and which, since the advent of cortisone, has become tractable; a victim of it can, with proper treatment, live out his allotted span of years. I asked Mrs. Oswald if she had meant this when she had spoken of "Atkinson's disease." Once again she found my interruption footling and answered simply, "Whatever," and put me down along with her coffee cup, which she returned to its saucer.

"As I was saying, as we all know, Lee Harvey Oswald, after leaving the Texas Book Depository, got off the bus and got into a taxi. This was right by the Greyhound bus station. Isn't it a strong likelihood that he went into the bus station to make a telephone call to the people he was working with, to say the mercy killing had come off? Maybe he did, maybe he didn't. But if he was guilty, why didn't he get on a bus and get out of Dallas? This theory fits in with the other theory. So were they all subversive and in a plot? Or were they all humanitarian and in a plot? The same people, though."

I wondered if, in my musings on her lares and penates when she was in the kitchen, I had missed the exposition of "this theory" and "the other theory," and rather tentatively, apologetic for my slow-wittedness, I asked, "The same people? Which people were these?"

"*They*," said Mrs. Oswald, and shook hands with herself for emphasis. "When I say *they*, I'm gonna quote Mrs. Kennedy when her husband was killed. She said, '*They* have killed my Jack,' and I say *they* in the same text. *They*, who are *they?* Ah! I have my own theory, and I'm sure everybody else has. There was one or two others that I can't recall at the moment to say '*they*.' I think Governor Connally said, '*They* are going to assassinate us all.' It's always *they*."

My interviews with Mrs. Oswald took place in the third or fourth week of the derangements in the Dominican Republic, and just as, in reading the reports of those, I could not keep the dramatis personae on the proper sides (or on top of) the proper fences, so now "they" swarmed about me like gnats, midges, fruit flies, and sand fleas, impossible to differentiate. I could not find my way out of the buzzing mob, and so I bent my head and drank some coffee and closed my eyes and tried to concentrate.

"If my son was an agent of the United States, this should be known. I wonder why Chief Justice Warren had tears in his eyes when President Johnson asked him to head up this commission? I wonder why?" She meditated, reading her palms. "Did Chief Justice Warren have to whitewash something the public don't know about? Did he know my son was innocent? Who *used* my son? This is the question I must find the answer to. Research and research, until I can bring the truth to light. My son was killed on cue, and this I can prove. The television cameras were ready, and the TV directors gave the order. As I understand it, some very important men in the networks got in trouble, lost their jobs and everything. But that's beside the point. What I want to know is who used Lee Harvey Oswald?"

The question was rhetorical and was put to the audience out there beyond the footlights, but I countered it with another, "Do you have any idea?"

"I don't have an *idea*, I *know*," she said. "And of course when I find out who framed my son, then we can find out who killed Kennedy. I go a little different way than most of the books on who killed Kennedy. My theory is a little different, because *I* know who framed my son and *he* knows I know who framed my son."

"Is 'he' in Texas now?"

"I can divulge nothing on that score," she said

brusquely, but screwed up her eyes in a cordial grimace to show that she forgave my intrusion into something that was none of my beeswax. I backed out of this dead end and returned to the avenue of the past I had tried to guide her down before. I asked what Lee Harvey's hobbies had been as a child.

"He had a stamp collection," she said with a practiced smile, "and he loved to play Monopoly, which is a thinking game. So was stamps. He had a stamp collection. He loved to play chess, he was a very good chess player. And anything like that. So he was really a very busy little boy, and I don't see anything abnormal about any part of his life. He'd climb up on the roof to look at the stars, and I'd have to get the older boys to get him down, because he was interested in astronomy. Now I'm talking about a boy eight, nine, ten years old. And he loved, he just loved to read very deep books. He liked Darwin, Hemingway, Norman Vincent Peale. When he went to visit my sister, all she said she saw him read was comic books, and this is what she said to the Warren Commission. Well, that was true, and he did like comic books. Isn't that normal in a young boy? He loved to read about animals. He knew all about animals. You know they said he played hooky in New York, and he did, and then of course we had to go to the board several times because he was always picked up in the Bronx zoo. We only lived about two blocks from there, and this is where they would always find him, because he loved animals. Someone said, 'Well, at least it was educational.' I have to smile a little bit because boys do play hooky. I don't say it's the right thing to do, and I don't say children should do it, but I certainly don't think it's abnormal. Lee came home one day when we were in New York just about a week or so, and it was exactly the time he was supposed to get home from school and I had given him enough lunch money and always gave a few extra nickels, you know, in case they needed something or got lost on the subway. Now I had never been in the subway—we had been in New York just about one week and I had driven to New York with Lee. So he said, 'Mother, I didn't go to school today.' I said, 'You didn't? Where did you go?' 'Oh,' he said, 'I rode all around. I rode all day on the subway. I rode to Brooklyn, I went to Queens, blah, blah, blah.' Well, I'm smiling to myself because, there again, from Texas if you go a few miles you pay twenty-five cents for bus fare, and if you go a few miles further, you have to pay extra, so I think he's

pulling my leg. I'm going along with him, not saying a thing. So that afternoon we're having supper
and I said to his brother, John Edward, 'What do
you think? Lee didn't go to school today, he rode
the subway all day long.' And of course they're
grinning because I'm the fool and don't know it,
see? And this went on and on and finally John Edward said, 'Mother, he's telling the truth, he can
ride the subway all day for the same amount of
money.' Well, I didn't know that, but the point is
Lee was telling me he didn't go to school. Now, I
want to say this in defense of my son—let's have
some defense of Lee Harvey Oswald and his mother!
How many boys at age thirteen that play hooky
from school would come home from school and tell
his mother that he did so?

"Well, of course, he played hooky after that and
they cautioned me *and* they cautioned me, and
finally they brought us into court and Lee was
taken from me and he was placed in a children's
home. I think he was in the home five or six weeks
and that was Warwick—I think that was the name
of it, I'd have to check in the Warren Report. In
Brooklyn. After the assassination, all of this came
out, and that Lee needed psychiatric treatment and
so on and so forth, and that I refused and that—

well, this was a clue to the assassination. I would have to read you the Warren Commission Report on Lee's psychiatric treatment and tear it apart. Lies! I was never told my son needed psychiatric treatment, believe me. And this man, I forget his name, I stepped on his toes, and sometimes I wonder, did he hold it against me enough to harm my son? By the way, do you know that he is Mayor Wagner's right-handed man? How do you suppose he got from probation officer to an official capacity in New York State?"

This time she really seemed to want an answer, but since I did not know who Mayor Wagner's right-handed man was (didn't know who his southpaw was either), let alone what his credentials were, I had to let her down. In view of the mass of detail she had at her command and the dexterous use she made of it to fit her argument, I felt like a flop on a junior high debating team who hadn't a prayer of reaching the semifinals.

"I find these things very, very interesting," she said, "because as I'm researching Lee's life—and I'm not the only one—it looks as though this boy's life has been supervised. But if I stress this, they say, 'This woman is out of her mind. Let's put her in a mental institution.' Isn't it silly?"

She chuckled at the preposterous way of the world, sipped coffee and, changing from her official to her chatty voice, said, "Lee purely loved animals! With his very first pay he bought a bird and a cage, and I have a picture of it. He bought this bird with a cage that had a planter for ivy, and he took care of that bird and he made the ivy grow. Now, you see, there could be many nice things written about this boy. But, oh, no, no, this boy is supposed to be the assassin of a President of the United States, so he has to be a louse. Sometimes I am very sad."

I started to mouth some safe platitude of sympathy, but I got no further than an introductory mutter. She went right on. "When I think of all the things Lee did!" Her tranquillity was ruffled, and her voice went up a note or two; it was the voice of a woman in altercation with a butcher who had overcharged her or with someone who had jostled her in a bus. "How can you call him a loner or an introvert or whatever they wanted to call him? Of course after they arrested him they had to find an environmental factor, and right away they said we moved around a lot. Well, all right, what if we did? We weren't drifters. This is the twentieth century, and people move around. That's educational, isn't it? No matter where we were, we always had a decent home. I wouldn't put up with a piece of torn upholstery or something broken or anything like that—I'd go to the five-and-dime and get something and fix it up. You see how I live—nothing fancy, but a bright touch, a little decorator piece here and there." She waved both hands, gesturing toward the appointments of the room and bestowing her good wishes on them.

"And I never neglected my children. Oh, yes, we didn't have steak, but we never even thought about steak—I didn't anyway, I was always grateful to eat. And the children never really and truly complained. I know of one or two occasions when the boys said, 'Mother, why don't you have a platter of chops? I was at such and such a house yesterday and they served seconds,' and I said, 'Well, now, honey, this is all Mother can do.' If, say, three days before payday, I had a dollar and a half to my name, I would cook up a big pot of beans and cornbread or a big pot of spaghetti and meatballs and make it last, but I happen to know some women in that position who would take that dollar and a half and go to the corner restaurant and come home with hamburgers and Coke, and there's your difference. I have always done what I thought was right, and I always did it in a true Christian way. And even though we were poor and I was a widow and I did have to support myself and three children, I always seemed to manage. I have often been complimented about how I look when I'm dressed up, about my little home and about the way the children act and so on and so forth.

"Now I'm patting myself on the back as a mother only so that the people will understand. Why am I so concerned that the people will understand? It is natural because I am a mother in history. I am in twenty-six volumes of the Warren Report, which is all over the world, so I must defend myself and defend my son Lee."

She altered the position of a green glass ashtray in the shape of a swan. Then, as if she had given the matter sober thought and this was her considered opinion, she said, "I would say that the Oswald family was actually an average American family."

What the components were that made up Mrs. Oswald's image of "an average American family," I never learned. I asked, but the answer was apparently self-evident and she ignored me. Since I do not know either how the sociologists and statisticians arrive at this denomination, it is quite possible that she and her brood fitted into it. But certain eccentricities of their circumstance had struck me when I had read the acres of newsprint, following the assassination, and I doubted that the word "average" was precise, or even approximate. To begin with, the record of Mrs. Oswald's matrimonial misfortunes shoots off at a forty-five degree angle from the norm. She was abandoned by her first husband, Edward John Pic, when her child by him, John Edward, was an infant; she was widowed by Robert Lee Oswald when her first son by him was a child and Lee Harvey was not yet born. Her third marriage to a Mr. Eckdahl was a hurricane, and while the lull before it was lengthy ("I made him wait a year") and the restoration period afterward was long, the storm itself, which raised the roof under which they dwelt together, was brief. The household, therefore, was only sporadically manned by a man.

The Oswald economy was far from stable. Under the terms of the first divorce, Mr. Pic was required to contribute to the support of his son, and Mr. Oswald had insured his life for a nominal sum. But these were humble funds, and Mrs. Oswald, pressed and proud and energetic, went to work. The boys, in the absence of a full-time caretaker, were sent variously to schools and to church-sponsored children's homes. Lee Harvey joined his older brothers in a Lutheran orphanage when he was three. Sometimes they were at home with their mother, and when they were old enough, they got jobs to pay for their board and keep. (Robert Oswald, at sixteen, had a job as a shoe-stock boy at Everybody's Department Store.)

The family moved with dizzying frequency while they lived in New Orleans, and later on when they lived in and around Fort Worth. Sometimes they rented apartments and sometimes they owned houses; they appear very often to have lived in two-family dwellings; when she was unencumbered, Mrs. Oswald stayed in lodgings. In both cities, their addresses were in similar neighborhoods, and John Edward Pic and Robert Lee Oswald, in their testimony before the Warren Commission, had trouble remembering the names of the streets where they had lived. When I asked Mrs. Oswald where John Edward Pic had lived in New York at the time she and Lee Harvey stayed with him there for a short and troubled interval, she said she did not know, that he and his wife were "somewhere on the East side," giving me a choice ranging from Delancey Street to Spanish Harlem, with Sutton Place and Gracie Square in between. She was an urban product, the kind of person who knows her own neighborhood thoroughly, may know two or three neighborhoods thoroughly, but who has no sense of a city as a whole; the ambience of New York did not differ from that of New Orleans, nor did New Orleans differ from Fort Worth.[2]

Even as she sat in her own parlor with only me to stimulate her, she emanated restlessness; she fairly skipped as she was sitting down. She had handed down her energy and wanderlust to her sons, all of whom joined the Marines as early as they could. ("We are a military family," she said.) However, at the same time, nomadic as she was, her nest-building instinct was steadfast; but it was the instinct of a migratory species that insofar as possible duplicates in successive nests twigs and leaves from the same sorts of trees and swatches of the same kinds of moss and lichen. Nothing in the room appeared to have more than the most ephemeral association of time or place; whenever, in the course of my interviews, I asked where she had got a vase or a bowl or a tray, she said, "Oh, that's just a little decorator thing I picked up to go with the other colors."

Her sons, under her guidance, were upright.

[2] See Appendix II, page 119.

"They didn't cuss—of course I don't say they didn't
on the outside, but they didn't in front of me. We
none of us used obscene language—oh, I might say
'damn,' you know, some time, but none of the boys.
And one little thing I did with 'em—but they never
did know until later on in life—I never let them
have a key to the front door. I remember Robert
asking me and I said, 'Oh, no, honey, it's better you
wake me up because if I ever heard the front door
I would think it was a burglar or something.' But
this wasn't the idea. I wanted to be sure that no boy
of mine would come into my home drunk. And I
can truthfully say not a one of them ever entered
my home stinko. They probably had a beer on the
outside, for I'm not saying they're perfect. Now I
have no objection to social drinking and I've been
to cocktail parties myself, but I don't drink, because alcohol doesn't agree with me at all, but I
would if I wanted to. And another thing, I never
let my boys have my car, 'cause I thought they
were too young to use it, and as it was my livelihood,
as I was an insurance lady, I couldn't afford to let
a teen-ager wreck it. The teen-agers, as we say—I
think they're a wonderful bunch, but they were
going a little wild, had their own cars and so on
and so forth. So I never let my boys have my car,

29

and I can truthfully say, none of my boys ever came into my home drunk. I think this is a very nice thing to say, a woman raising children by herself, particularly boys. I'm gonna give myself credit for this, and I think I deserve it."

The room was still cool, but the air was heavy, imbued with the second-hand mustiness of air-conditioning and the smoke from my cigarettes. I was tired and headachy, but Mrs. Oswald was as fresh and kinetic as she had been when she greeted me, and she persevered like a long-distance runner.

"You know, there was a violent campaign against me as well as my son in magazines, newspapers, and written literature. Most all the papers pictured me in a sort of a bad light, but really I'm not that way at all and never was. I should say I'm very outspoken, I'm aggressive, I'm no dope. Let's face it, if you step on my toes I'm gonna fight back, and I don't apologize for that. This was my training along with Lee's father, who, as we all know, is now deceased."

(Although I should have been used to it by now, I was surprised each time she used the royal or tutorial "we," and only the most tenuous hold on reality kept me from glancing from left to right to see who besides me was attending the lecture.)

"When my older boy first went to school, he came home one day crying that the children had taken his pennies away from him. Mr. Oswald took his little hand and started teaching him how to fight back, and I listened and I thought it was a wonderful thing. I remember him saying 'If you ever start a fight, you're gonna be whipped, but if they ever start a fight with you and you don't fight back, I'm gonna whip *you*.' Let me give you one little instance with Lee and the next-door neighbor boy. They were approximately the same age, and if not, they were the same height, and Lee had a dog. He loved his shepherd collie dog. It was named Sunshine. He used to romp in the back yard with his dog and took him every place he went, and this little boy was throwing rocks over the fence at Lee's dog. Well, my kitchen window had a view to the back yard. And I watched my son Lee for approximately three days telling the little boy over the fence he better stop throwing rocks at his dog. Well, I was amused, and I was just waiting to find out what happened. Finally, one day when I came home from work the father called me on the phone. It seemed his son was very badly beaten up—in a child's way. My son Lee had finally taken upon himself, after much patience, I thought, to confront the little boy enough to fight him, and the father didn't approve. I told the father what happened, and since the boys were approximately the same age and height, let them fight their own battles.

"Now my boys were never tied to my apron strings. And Lee, Lee wanted to know all there was about life. Talking about going to Russia. He never did tell me why he went to Russia. I have my own opinion. He spoke Russian, he wrote Russian, and he read Russian. Why? Because my boy was being trained as an agent, that's why. Another thing I found out in some book where it said he was placed in another hut because he couldn't get along with someone. He was placed with a Cuban, and he was learning Spanish. I think he was spying on that Cuban. It's just so obvious. How many Marines are going around reading Russian and getting Russian newspapers? One and one make two to me. That boy was being trained."

I asked her what she thought Lee would have done with his life if he had not been killed, and she answered at once, as if she had answered the question many times before. "From what I know of my boy, and of course you have to understand that actually the last time I was very close to Lee was before he joined the service in 1956. After that, it was just through correspondence and on his leaves home from the Marines that I knew him. But every time he came home he talked and talked about the Marines and nothing else. I know when he came back from Japan he said, 'Oh, what a wonderful experience, what a wonderful trip!' He said, 'Do you know it cost my government over two thousand dollars to send me there? I could never afford it on my own.' I think he was doing with his life what he wanted to do. And I'm gonna say he was working for his country as an agent. I think that at age sixteen he became involved, that at age sixteen Lee Harvey Oswald was being trained as a government agent. And this brings up Russia and, of course, Marina."

I was glad she had broached the subject of her daughter-in-law. I had been shy of doing so myself because I knew that there was bad blood between the two women.

"Let's have some more coffee before I go into that," she said. "We'll *need* it." She went once again to the kitchen, where, with her back to me as she went about the business of the coffee, she honed her scalpels for the vivisection of Marina.

"Of course I don't know too much about Marina. She lived with me the one month when they came

3 3

back from Russia. She was a very humble foreign girl, and she never smoked in front of me. Everything was 'Momma' and the baby, and we got along fine. Now this person never smoked in front of me for a reason, because she did smoke, and she smoked in Russia. The testimony of the Presidential report showed that she knew Americans before she knew Lee, and they taught her how to smoke. Now I smoked for twenty years, and Lee never did say a word to me about smoking—maybe he had respect because I was a mother. But he objected to his wife smoking. And she evidently thought I never smoked, because she never smoked in front of me. I didn't know Marina smoked, until the assassination."

(At the moment, like a white rat in some unprecedented experiment, I had a lighted cigarette in my hand, and another was burning in the ashtray.)

"And you see, I wouldn't be that type. I would be natural and do what I have to do, and there again we get into she's not a true person. If I smoke, I smoke in front of everybody. Of course, I would ask permission of an older person."

There was a moment's silence, and I tried to remember if I had minded my manners at the beginning and asked if I could smoke; I thought I

had, but at this point I could be sure of nothing
except that I was a white rat.

"To me, Marina is not a true person," she said
with fair-minded deliberation. "And this is hard
to explain. I have to ask myself who Marina Oswald really is. I'd like to see her marriage certificate
some time, and I'd like to know more about her. Oh,
when Marina went to Washington, Washington
fell in love with Marina Oswald, and Chief Justice
Warren was her grandfather, but when I went to
Washington—'Don't listen to her. Momma hadn't
seen Lee in a year, and she doesn't know anything, blah, blah, blah.' Everything was against
me. Yet *I* was the mother. Now I don't say that
Marina is necessarily guilty of anything, but both
she and Mrs. Paine have lied, lied continuously.
Maybe they are not guilty, but why is it necessary
to lie? When it first happened, Marina did not
identify the rifle. She said, 'Yes, Lee had rifle,' but
when they showed it to her she said she couldn't
say whether that was his. Now this is understand-
able. If your husband had a rifle, and particularly
if he had it as they say he had it, wrapped up in a
blanket and never using it, would the wife be able
to identify it? Yet a few weeks later, when she had
taken oath and been brainwashed by the Secret

35

Service, she identified the rifle as Lee's. And at first she said, 'Lee good man, Lee no shoot anybody.' And then she changed her testimony. Marina seems French to me."

"French!"

"Yes, sweetheart, that's what I said, Marina Oswald seems French to me. Oh, definitely." She came back with our coffee, and as she put it down beside me, she said, "But that will have to be continued in our next. You'll have to drink up, honey, your driver's here."

I had not heard a car, and shrubbery obscured the window that looked onto the street, but when I peered through the interstices of the privet, I saw that she was indeed right and the car to take me back to Dallas, where I was staying, was at the curb. I began to respect the sixth sense she had several times laid claim to. ("I have a very unusual extrasensory perception," she had said once, "so doesn't it stand to reason that if my boy shot the President I would have *known* at the time it happened?") I respected, also, her dramatic sense of timing, and I wondered how I would hang to the cliff until I heard about Marina's French origins.

As I got up to go, I asked if she would object to my bringing a tape recorder the following day; she said that, on the contrary, she would be glad if I did, if, that is, I brought two machines, since she wanted one tape to preserve "for history." She had made many recordings, she told me, for "mass mediums" and for her own purposes; she knew that she spoke at the rate of a hundred and eighty words a minute, and I was to tell that to the man I rented the machines from. An operator would not be necessary, because she knew how "to work 'em all."

I started toward the bedroom to fetch my Neiman-Marcus rain cape, and my eye drifted willy-nilly toward the scroll over the desk. I did not look at it directly but instead at a tempera on wood of a baroque orange and chestnut newel post (a detail from backstairs at Blenheim Castle? from Marion Davies' house?), which she dismissed: "A little decorator thing. I thought it would go with the chair. But now this, this is important, this is what you should see," and she took the scroll down from its hook.

"I was gonna show you this," she said. "Here, the man can wait—I guess he's getting paid, isn't he? You get out your notebook and copy it down, and be sure you get the words right."

The legend, cut into copper, read,

MY SON—

LEE HARVEY OSWALD EVEN AFTER HIS
DEATH HAS DONE MORE FOR HIS COUNTRY
THAN ANY OTHER LIVING HUMAN BEING
                    MARGUERITE C. OSWALD

As I was writing down this abstruse manifesto
(I could not get a purchase on the syntax), Mrs.
Oswald brought my things and smiled disarmingly.
"Of course, I'm not a writer like you," she said.
"But I like how that sounds. That's what I said at
the year period when I went to the grave. Newspaper reporters came by the galore and asked if I
had anything to say, and I said this. And every
word of it is true. I'm proud of my son, and why
not? My son is an unsung hero."

I remembered that she had petitioned to have
Lee Harvey buried in Arlington Cemetery.

I thanked her for giving me so much of her time,
and I thanked her for the coffee. Her handclasp was
firm and straightforward, and her eyes shone with
zeal and satisfaction and optimism. "We're going
to win in the end."

I was not sure whether the "we" was editorial
or whether I had now been initiated into a coterie
whose adversaries were "they."

On the drive back, I browsed through some matter Mrs. Oswald had lent me. One was a paperback book by Kerry Thornley, who had known Lee Harvey in the Marines and had dedicated his "iconoclastic critique on how America helped Oswald to become what he did" to "Clint Bolton, who first said to me: 'Go home and write—ya bum!' " I did not get much further than that. The other was a pamphlet proving that it was ballistically impossible for Oswald to have killed Kennedy; this was a compilation of diagrams and of copies of letters that had been sent, accompanying the diagrams, to leading magazines and to people of position—the letters, significantly, had gone unanswered or had been brushed aside; a ferocious admonition in the beginning of the text prevents me from quoting any part of it.

Soon after the assassination, my husband got a good many letters addressed to him in his role as critic of the press; most of them told him how to go about his reporting, and most of them went into the wastepaper basket. He was, as a matter of fact, at work on one of his "Wayward Press" analyses for *The New Yorker* just before he died, a little more than a month after the President was killed. He brought home for me to read one of the letters, whose author implored, "Mr. Liebling, go to Dallas and tell us the truth. You might of course get killed in Texas, but if you get killed, the world shall know that somebody from the right (be it Birchers or Southern Democrats) wants to hide the truth."

Exegetes of the Dallas murders sprang up like mushrooms in a pinewoods after a soaking rain; the mycelium at the round earth's four corners was rich and ready. Many of the toadstools that appeared were harmless but without flavor, some were tasty and even delicious, many more were as noxious as the amanita verna. In the cities, in whose purlieus these mycologists' wonderlands flourished, kangaroo courts met round the clock, and some of the judges and some of the jurors were responsible people, and the opinions they handed down were persuasive. They were shooting in the dark, but they managed to convince themselves and millions of others that their shots dispelled the darkness and everything was limpidly illuminated; theory, creative and flexible, made mincemeat of circumstantial evidence. The name of the prisoner in the dock was legion; he had every pigmentation and every shape of jaw known to anthropology; he was a member of every political organization, every religious fraternity, every business, scientific, criminal, occult conclave of every country on the face

of the earth. In some of these courtroom spectacu-
lars (the remarks from the peanut gallery were
deafening; the confusion was such that one could
not remember which were the good guys and which
the bad ones among Mark Lane, Perry Mason,
Melvin Belli, and *The Defenders'* man, let alone
which belonged to the bar association and which to
the American Federation of Radio and Television
Artists), Lee Harvey Oswald was convicted of having pulled the trigger, *but* at the instigation of a
highly organized and dangerous gang; in other re-
enactments of the drama, he was not even on the
premises, but was under a haystack, fast asleep. In
Europe, where there has never been an assassination of a political figure for an apolitical, individual
reason, the idea that Oswald, obscure, untutored,
could have acted on his own was insupportable, and
the most important papers of the most important
capitals carried stories categorically proving conspiracy.

As we entered Dallas and drove along the route of
the President's caravan, I observed, as I had the
other two times I had been over this same ground,
that the distance between the sixth-floor window
of the Texas Book Depository and the place where
the car, slowing for a turn, had been, seemed to be

much less than it had appeared in photographs. I was struck, moreover, by the fact that between the window and the target there was no obstruction of any kind to challenge aim or deflect the attention, no eave or overhang or tree. The drop shot, from a steadied rifle, was fired on a day of surpassing clarity; the marksmanship of the gunner did not have to be remarkable.

II

II

Having taken Mrs. Oswald at her word, I refused the offer of a lesson in manipulation when the man delivered the tape recorders to my hotel. This was unwise; despite her boast that she could work 'em all, Mrs. Oswald couldn't work these, and I had never clapped eyes on a tape recorder before in my life. After a quarter of an hour of bungling experimentation, plugging and unplugging, punching buttons and shifting levers, reversing bobbins, profitlessly studying instructions that might as well have been written in Arabic (and possibly were), we were both exasperated. Sitting on the floor with our hair awry, amid furniture that we had dislodged in our futile fiddling, we were exasperated with the contraptions and with each other. Mrs.

Oswald said with some asperity that these were inferior machines, that I should not have cut corners when matters of such importance were at stake (I felt as defensive as if the machines belonged to me; I wanted to invent an affidavit from *Consumer Reports* to fling before her), but, having chosen to do so, I should have learned how to run the trashy thingumbobs. She went to the bedroom to telephone the shop to ask for help, and while she was gone, Lady Luck visited me in a dazzling revelation and piloted my fingers in a virtuoso performance, unique in my experience, so that when she came back with the disgruntling news that since it was Saturday the shop was closed, I was delighted to point to the smoothly revolving wheels. (In that moment I became eight years old, and, having just outwitted one of my smug older sisters, it was all I could do to keep from yammering like a monkey.)

"Well, now! If we just keep at a thing, we'll get it to go in the end, isn't that the truth?" she cried, pleased with her stick-to-itiveness, which had borne practical fruit as well as an opportunity to express an eternal verity. "Oh, I can tell we'll work well together! Right here it's proved that together we're a mechanical genius."

We stationed ourselves, I in the chair where I had sat the day before and Mrs. Oswald beneath Whistler's old lady.

She picked up her microphone and spoke into it clearly. Because she never groped for a word and because her undertones and overtones and rhythms altered at such cleverly strategic times, I, the only visible member of her audience, was caught up and indoctrinated even when I heard grumblings from the back of the house that her arguments were specious, her logic bizarre, and her deductions plucked from the foggy, foggy air.

"Now about Marina being a true or untrue picture," she said, stating the text for the day. "Marina, as I have said, seems French to me. I have researched everything about Marina over and over. When she went to New Orleans, she did not want to live in an apartment with high ceilings. Now where does she know about the high ceilings? There may be a simple answer for this and all the other things, but I don't have it, and I want it. And she complained about the cockroaches, which is all right, but a foreign girl knows how to clean up things. And then, of course, she knew a little French too."

Considering that she was French, the fact that

she knew a little French too must have been useful.

"There's one letter in the Warren Report from Russia from Lee that said he married this girl and she spoke a little French. Well, the letters had to be retyped because they didn't photograph well, and they omitted the word French. If you use a magnifying glass and look at Lee's letter, you will see that Marina speaks a little French. Now I ask myself: was this deliberate, or was this just an error? But when you find so many errors and so much coincidence, then you begin to wonder if something's being whitewashed and if there isn't something more to it than meets the eye.

"And Marina knew English. Marina and I conversed. I don't know Russian and this is the part that I was indignant about. Because after she went to live with Mr. Martin in his home with his family they put her on television, and that day she spoke real well broken English. If they said she didn't know English, that's baloney. She could understand, but when she went out any place she didn't open her mouth and she made out she didn't speak or understand English. This is what I mean when I say she is not a true person."

"But why do you think she's French?" I insisted, not at all satisfied with the proposition that an

aversion to high ceilings and cockroaches was idio-
pathically Gallic.

"I wish I could go into this, I truly do, but it's
just like 'how do I love you?' It's just something
that doesn't make sense, you know, and you know
it. I felt this almost when I first met her and saw
that she didn't look Russian. She doesn't look Russian at all."

I recalled that when I had seen the first photographs of Marina, I had been reminded of the
flawed beauty of the girls in the Soviet films of a
few years ago—the imperfections of skin and teeth
of Veronica in *The Cranes Are Flying* had been in-
explicably touching. Today, Oswald's widow is
much different, cropped and kempt and "styled,"
but at the time no face had looked to me more
Chekhovian or Dostoevskian or Pushkinesque—she
could have been Lisa in *Pique Dame*, destined to
hurl herself into the Neva as the sad snow fell all
around her, or Masha, of all the three sisters the
one most given to tears.

Mrs. Oswald, however, stated unequivocally, "She
looks French," and that was that. "Now the only
thing I'm *sure* of is that *I* had nothing to do with
the assassination. I'm not sure about anybody else.
And because I am looking for the truth, everyone

is under suspicion in a way. You see, I don't know who's who. I have to evaluate everybody, and Marina doesn't ring true. Of course, I never hear anybody else say she was French. But I have my reasons for saying this, which will be very delicate. She doesn't ring true, to begin with, in respect to motherhood. Even if she thinks in her mind that Lee was guilty, the thing to do was protect him for her children's sake and for her sake—no, I'm not talking about lying, because I don't believe in lying, but I mean, to give out stories like if she had met him outside Russia she would never have married him, because of the type he was and so on and so forth. That's just downing him more and more, and yet she's the mother of his children. This is not true of motherhood or womanhood. Even if he was a louse, she would defend him to a certain extent. She never goes out to the cemetery. She did in the very beginning. She went out, and everything was fine, and then when she was taken over she started changing. And whether it was for the security of the country, whether this was her role, whether she's being threatened, which is a possibility—whatever reason, it's not a nice reason, and this is why she is not a true person. First she says, 'Lee good man, Lee no shoot anybody,' and everything was in Lee's favor, and then all of a sudden they get aholt of her and put her on television and she says she thinks in her mind her husband is guilty, and from then on her husband's a louse. These are the things that just don't jive.

"And now another thing, all the witnesses told how she started complaining about everything as soon as she got here, how she treated him and how she talked about her sexual life and how she denounced him and so on and so forth, and taking up with these Russian people. This is all in black and white. I'm not imagining these things, and thank God there are other people taking this up. I say thank God because there some people who would like to think that I have hallucinations—I know it's already been said in the Warren Report. It was said by some attorney. Point blank. 'Do you think your sister'—they said this to my sister—'do you think that your sister has hallucinations?' Why? Because I notice the inaccuracies and coincidences and things that don't jive? I know some people who wouldn't hesitate to make a mental case outa me, and believe me, if anybody's in their right mind, it's Mrs. Marguerite Oswald."

She paused to let this sink in and take root, and, as she did so, looked me in the eye.

51

"No matter what Marina does, it's news, but locally I can show reporters something in black and white and they won't give me coverage. This is the difference. This is where the human element comes in. And this is where I have been persecuted and have suffered just like my son. Oh, I can hear the 'ah's' when they read this—here is Miz Oswald feeling sorry for herself. No, no, I'm not feeling sorry for myself, but I know for a fact that I have been persecuted. What's wrong with Miz Oswald? Why does she think she's being persecuted? Is she mentally unbalanced? I have been asked that question publicly. No, no. Without persecution, there wouldn't be a persecution complex. This is what Freud[1] said himself. Shut off your tape, dearheart."

I did as I was told, anticipating a confidence too sensitive or hazardous to national security to be recorded, but all she said was, "Don't you think it's too hot for coffee today? Let me make you a glass of iced tea. I've got some nice Indian iced tea with a kind of a spicy flavor."

Today she was wearing a blue denim jumper and a perky red and white striped shirt, and she was shod in sneakers. She looked as carefree and fun-loving as the wife of the man in the ad who

[1] See Appendix III, page 120.

has retired to Florida at the age of fifty, thanks to having taken the advice of his farsighted insurance broker. I felt that she should have been telling me more about the iced tea, but even as she emptied ice trays clamorously and rattled spoons, she rode her tempest. "Maybe you saw where Marina was offered ten thousand dollars for the guns? The gun that killed President Kennedy and the telescope sight that went with it and the gun that killed Tippit?"

I said that I had. I had been dumfounded, as a matter of fact, that the weapons had not been acquired by the FBI or by the Smithsonian Institution, but I had been reminded that they belonged to the dead man's estate and were now Marina's to dispose of as she wished. The story I had read said that a "private collector" was negotiating for them, and at the time I had wondered what manner of man he could be.

"Well, now, let me tell you about Marguerite Oswald being a mental case. When I read that, I said to myself, now those guns are worth a great deal more than ten thousand dollars and Marina should get more money for my grandchildren. I am thinking about *my* grandchildren. So I called the Fort Worth *Star Telegram* and told them what I thought. I said, 'Those guns are priceless, but if they're gonna be sold, let's see some justice done to the children of Lee Harvey Oswald.' And just last week there was an item in the Fort Worth *Star Telegram* that said a Frenchman had offered twenty thousand."

(Later on that evening, back in Dallas, a newspaper reporter told me that the second offer had been topped and that Marina had received five thousand on account and that forty thousand more was being held for her in escrow until the estate was settled. Since that time, the picture has changed altogether.) [2]

"So, you see, I do my bit. But nobody knows, and it's a shame they don't. I'm not unhappy. You can see I'm not, can't you? But I'm a mother in history, I'm all over the world. There's two Presidents in my life, and *my* son's the one accused. You know, here is Mrs. Kennedy, a very wealthy woman, Mrs. Tippit, a very wealthy woman, Marina, very wealthy, but *I* am wondering where my next meal is coming from. It's almost unbelievable, it's sometimes almost like a spiritual."

She brought me a dewy glass of tea with a spray

[2] See Appendix IV, page 121.

of fresh mint. It was sugary and rather good, and
it had no taste of tea.

"Here we are, we four women in history, and
yet *I* am the mother. But has anyone come forward to reimburse me for my emotional stability?
No, no! And I have given of time and my voice, yet
I have twenty-three hundred dollars to my name.
I'm not complaining. I have my health. I eat well,
I'm not brooding. But isn't it strange? Now I made
a television interview with Belli in Los Angeles, and
we were so good they wouldn't stop the cameras
but wanted us to go on for an hour instead of the
half hour. And I got one hundred dollars for that.
Yet Richard Burton was on the same program the
next night and he got *five thousand* dollars. What
do you think he did with it? He gave it to charity.
He is not even an American, yet he gave it to
charity, and here is Mrs. Oswald, the mother, talking and talking about the American way of life, and
where's the rent money coming from? You understand I don't care about money. Money is only good
to its use, but I need money to carry on the campaign against the campaign against me, and as a
mother, I think I deserve it. I got fired from my
job as practical nurse because of the assassination,
and it broke my heart. I didn't make only five dol-

lars a week, but I was glad to work for that because I was doing it for humanity."

"Five dollars a week?" I asked, wondering what part of the century she had flashed back to.

"Sometimes five, sometimes twenty-five. Seven days a week helping people. I was fired because of the assassinating, yet I was only the mother. Six months later when I went in the clothes locker I saw my uniform and shoes and everything and I just broke down. It just hit me hard. But now I have accepted this, and I feel like now I would never like to nurse again. I just don't feel like I would like to go into anybody else's sorrow. I have enough of my own. It's a hard life. Why, the very day of the assassination I was nursing and I heard it on the radio, that my son, Lee Harvey Oswald had been taken into custody. I came right home and called the Fort Worth *Star Telegram* and asked them to send over a press car to take me to Dallas. You can push the button on again. We can drink our tea and talk at the same time. Is there anything you want to ask me?"

"Yes, there is," I said. "When did you last see Lee?"

"I saw Lee in the jailhouse after the assassination, and he was all bruised up with black eyes and all and I said, 'Honey, did they beat you?' and he said, 'It isn't anything, Mother. I just got in a scuffle.' Now this is normal, he wouldn't tell his mother if he had been mistreated by the police. But I have my opinion."

"But before the assassination? How long had it been since you'd seen him?"

"I hadn't seen Lee since October, the end of October, 1962. Just about a year, that would make it. I used to do live-ins and sometimes I'd be two hundred miles away, but the truth is, Lee and Marina left Fort Worth and didn't even tell me where they were. I called Robert and he said Lee had a box number on him and I told Robert to make sure he took care of his brother and so on. I was not in a position financially to help, working the way I was. And another thing, I was a little miffed. They left without telling me they were leaving. I was there that afternoon, and they left the next morning, and there's more to it than that, but never mind. And I thought, well, when they get good and ready they'll come and see me. I hadn't seen John Edward for years before, or Robert either, and I felt, well, I'm their mother and when they get ready it's their place to come and see me. I don't worry about them any more. And this was

the attitude I took with Lee and Marina. They
lived with me for a month and then they moved
out. I'm a working person, I have to pay my own
rent, make my own living, and I don't have the
money or the time to run back and forth and they
didn't have a car to come over here. You understand? And, too, I wouldn't have a place to put
them up if they came to visit me. Maybe if I
had a three-bedroom house. Maybe then they'd
take the bus and come over for the weekend,
but I never was in that position. I am entirely
alone. I do not have even my children to discuss things with. For instance, Lee was left-handed,
and right away I realized whoever shot the gun,
it would make a difference. So I called Robert
and he wouldn't answer these important questions.
I have suffered very much."

Although Mrs. Oswald frequently made state-
ments like this, designed to cause the blood of her
interlocutor to run cold with embarrassment and
to immobilize the tongue, such was the self-pro-
tecting and even complacent nature of her hostility
to the world at large and to Washington in particular that she did not urge (indeed, she did not invite)
one to enter her Castle Rackrent to view each tribu-
lation separately. Rather, it was as if she had posted

a notice on the door that read "Black Death" or "Beware of the Snakes," to indicate that inside there was mortification so monstrous and esoteric and ineradicable, and, paradoxically, so precious, that it could not be taken in by any ordinary intelligence. I was guilty, I had contributed my galling bit to this treasure house of anguish and humiliation, but so had everybody else on earth.

Serenely she spoke to the microphone, smiling now and then in composure as she tallied some of life's ironies, arching her dark eyebrows in astonishment at some of the most "spiritual" aspects of "The Case."

"You know, it's a strange thing, a very interesting thing the way things have happened to me all my life. I said it's sometimes like a spiritual and I say it again. Now ever since right before the Warren Report came out, the Fort Worth *Star Telegram* wrote they would not run a thing on the assassination—they had had a big dose, a big dose of castor oil. I asked why wasn't the *Star Telegram* carrying any of my quotes—the Dallas reporters and everybody else was out at the cemetery for the year period—*they* wanted to hear from me and I was on television and all, but there wasn't a thing said in the local paper about me being out at the cemetery for the year period. And of course there were things said about the Tippits and the Kennedys, and I asked this young reporter, and he said, 'Miz Oswald, they had a big dose here.'

"But let's go back a little bit and I'll give you an example of the way things have always worked against me. I used to work in Algiers, Louisiana, during the war, and that is across the river from New Orleans. I was a switchboard operator. My duty was six o'clock in the morning until three or six-thirty, I forget which. So I rented a room in Algiers, Louisiana, and my sister was taking care of Lee permanently at this particular time. He was about two years old. Every evening I left Algiers and took the ferry and came over and took care of my baby, and would have to leave early enough to get home before dark—after all, I was a woman alone—to be across the river so I could go to work for six-thirty. And the Naval Base personnel used to come with a jeep to pick me up because there was no other way to get to the Naval Base. Well, this was typical of most of my life. It's a little humorous in a way, but it's typical of things that have happened to me right along. I was on this side of New Orleans and this young lady that also roomed where I was rooming had a car and she

was coming to New Orleans and she told me that
if I would stay over she would take me home. Well,
my two nephews had had a tonsillitis operation and
I went to the hospital and stayed a little while with
them and then I met this young lady and she had
a date and they decided that we should go into one
of the nightclubs in the Vieux Carré and have a
little recreation. Well, now I love to dance and go
out to dinner and places like that, and so I said I
would.

"And before I knew it, it was two o'clock in
the morning. What could I do? I'm with them, they
have the car, so I have to wait. So when I did get
home I called the other young lady who worked
the evening shift for the switchboard and told her
I wasn't feeling well and would she take the morning and I would take the evening. She said she
would. However, it didn't please her too much. So
that afternoon I was called to the Colonel's office
and he asked me what happened and I told him I
wasn't feeling well, and that I had been up until
late and had been to the hospital—that part of
course was true—so it was perfectly natural that
I call the other young lady and ask her to change
with me.

"However, I did dance, you see, with a few of

the boys, and they happened to be men from the base, but how was I to know that? And he told me that I was not telling the truth and that I had been seen in a nightclub and I was dancing until two o'clock in the morning when I should have been home in bed resting to be there for the six o'clock shift. And he fired me, right then and there."

She allowed the climax to remain frozen for a moment before she rang the curtain down to point the moral. "This is just a little story that shows what goes on in my life. I was fired right on the spot! When I think of all the things that are being said about me, I think about all these things that have happened, and there must be a simple explanation for them. It is my job to *find* that explanation for all the inaccuracies and distortions and so on and so forth so that the people will understand."

I asked only one more question that day, and I did so with trepidation. I asked if she had voted in the last Presidential election. She bridled, but her outrage was put on like a false nose.

She said, "Why, honey, you know I can't discuss my personal politics. After all, I *am* responsible for two Presidents."

She took off the nose and meandered on. She

bemoaned the loss of mementos of Lee. "Lee was a beautiful child, and this is why I gave all the pictures of him to the magazines. I got rooked financially, but that was all right because they showed a nice clean boy and a boy not underfed. But I don't have many mementos for this reason: when Lee and Marina returned from Russia, I did as I did with the other boys as soon as they were married. I gave Lee his baby book and things of that kind, and Marina has them all now and refuses to give them to me. I gave Lee a watch that belonged to his father that was in my possession for years and years and years. It was a pocket watch and my husband was called after the General Robert E. Lee, but he was always called Lee. You see, my first son by Mr. Oswald is named Robert E. Lee and then Lee is called Lee. When Lee was born—that is, Lee Harvey Oswald—I never could say the name Lee because my husband was always called Lee. Am I making it plain?"

(No, but go on.)

"He was really named after the General, so I kept the watch for Lee. I had it all those years and then I gave it to Lee when he returned from Russia. I feel like these things are mine and I want them, but I have been very unsuccessful in

63

getting them back. Also, there is a little navy blue wool suit that the three boys wore and I have carried that around for over twenty-six years and it didn't even have a moth hole in it. It was an adorable little suit. Lee's picture in *Life*—'Evolution of an Assassin'—at six months has the suit on, and I gave it to my daughter-in-law, Robert's wife, just about three months before the assassination because I was nursing and moving around and I asked her to keep it for me. And that has not been returned to me. Actually, I have suffered a great deal."

The refrain, annunciating travail, came off with her customary unwavering matter-of-factness.

Among her souvenirs of Lee, Mrs. Oswald did still have a "little replica of a Magnus organ that I bought him while we were in New York for Christmas, 1953. I paid, let's see, I paid approximately $39.95 for it." This and other properties to whose sentimental value had been added a historic dimension, she kept in storage.

She spoke of letters she had written to prominent people when Lee was in Russia. "Here is a young boy, and let's say he was adventurous or anything about him, but anyhow he was in Russia trying to renounce his citizenship. Instead of blasting him on the front pages, why didn't they get together and see that he came home to his native land? I sent a telegram to the Mayor of Fort Worth, but I didn't receive an answer. I wrote to Sam Rayburn and to Christian Herter—I wonder what become of those letters? I also wrote to Mr. Khrushchev, July 19, 1960. I stated that Lee had gone to Russia in September of 1959 and that I had one letter from him in January, but my letter to him was returned and I never heard from him again. I asked Mr. Khrushchev to supply me with any information about his whereabouts, if he was working and so on and so forth, I said that I was much worried and deeply concerned as a mother would be.

"Now I did not receive an answer from Mr. Khrushchev, and this brings up another interesting aspect of the case. The letter to Christian Herter and the letter to Sam Rayburn and the letter to Congressman Jim White all expressed the same thing. I said from what I had read in the newspaper, my son said that he wanted to live in a Communist country, in a working man's country because of the Communists here and hate and racial discrimination and everything. And I made it perfectly plain that as an individual, even though he was young,

he had served in the Marines and he had became
an adult, not in age but in maturity because of his
hitch in the Marines, and as an individual, if this
was what he wanted to do I in no way wanted to influence him because I thought he had a right to his
own life, and this I believe. Yet Representative
Ford had a big article in *Life* magazine about
'Mother's Myth, Son an Agent,' and he must have
—or he *should* have known that I in no way wanted
to influence my son to come home. He said that I
went to Washington in 1961, which I did, when
I was in dire need, which I was, but I went to
petition President Kennedy to get my son to come
home in order to support and help me, *not* to influence him. What an injustice to a mother!"

In the most abrupt and perfunctory parenthesis
possible, she said that it was time for more iced tea,
and, raising her voice above the chattering of the
ice cubes as she briskly stirred our glasses of strange
brew, she lectured and invoked and apostrophized
without transition and with a grand if confounding
disregard for chronology. Immediately after she
had served up Representative Ford's head on a
platter, she took the Secret Service to task.

"The Secret Service would not let me get near

my daughter-in-law. I fought and fought like a wild animal. I called the head of the Secret Service I guess every day, begging to see my daughter-in-law, and they wouldn't let me get near her. So she changed her testimony. First it was, 'Lee was good man, Lee no do nothing, Lee no kill nobody.' And then I was pushed out, absolutely pushed out, and Marina Oswald's husband was a louse. Now I arrived in Dallas on March the ninth at the height of the Ruby trial and was told by reporters, and I can verify this, that Mrs. Paine was in Marina's house, but the point I'm going to make and make strongly is that I do not think it was fair that Mrs. Paine spoke with Marina Oswald before Mrs. Paine herself testified. Now I didn't have that opportunity, or my sons. I had never talked to John Edward or Robert or Marina or vice versa, so no one in the close family knew what each other was going to say. And this is very sad because we could have understood each other a little better, rather than bog each other down, as it came out some time. But Mrs. Paine did have that privilege to talk to my daughter-in-law, and this I don't like. This I don't like one bit. Why do the Secret Service let this strange woman see my daughter-in-law, and not me? But the Secret Service never questioned me, nor the FBI either. The Secret Service and the FBI never came near me."

"But you *have* been interviewed?" I said because there had flashed before my inward eye newspaper stories about her without number.

"Oh, yes, yes, of course I've been interviewed by the newspapers, if that's what you mean," she said crossly, still put out by having been given the cold shoulder by the FBI and the Secret Service. "I've been interviewed by *them* by the galore. Now let you give me an instance of how I hold a lot of these cards that will show up the inaccuracies and the errors. About the diary—you asked about that."

I had not asked about the diary; in fact, I had forgotten its existence. Possibly the question had come from someone nearer the front of the house.

"It has never been verified how the diary was leaked. It said in one article that no one knew where the diary came from, but a certain reporter in Dallas interviewed the widow, Mrs. Marina, quite often, so it implied that this is where the diary came from. And he refused to release where it came from. But she and her attorney expressed indignation about the release of the diary and so on, and they sent telegrams to the Warren Commission say-

ing they didn't think it was right, and the Warren
Commission was going to investigate, and the FBI.
So I just sat and waited. I smile inwardly quite a
bit when I read about myself. I smile and say, 'Oh,
goodness, how can you be so wrong?' Only way I
can survive, to have a little sense of humor.

"So I was smiling and waiting—this is good—
all this the FBI's going to check, you know. I'm
waiting and waiting, but no one came, so after the
third day I called the FBI, which is in Dallas, and
I forget the man's name and I told him who I was
and I said, 'You know I have been waiting for
someone to come over and question me about the
release of the so-called diary. And nobody has.' And
he said, 'Well, do you have the diary, Miz Oswald?'
And I said, 'No, I don't, but I just can't imagine
all the fuss about the diary and not coming and
asking if I released the diary.' He said, 'They didn't
come because they knew you didn't have it.' And
I said, 'Yes, they know I didn't have it because
they released it *themelves!*' Now do you get an
idea of what I'm talking about? Why, I mean, this
just insults my intelligence."

For one second I was carried back in time to a
winter when I had been a student at the University
of Heidelberg. One afternoon an American friend

and I were moseying through Woolworth's on the Hauptstrasse (we found this a good way to pick up the German words for miscellaneous hardware) when we saw a Japanese student at the stationery counter having a plainly fruitless conversation with the clerk. My friend Hightower (now a distinguished sinologist at Harvard) had a smattering of Japanese and was as much impelled, I think, to show it off as he was to do a good turn. The Japanese was grateful—he had wanted gummed reinforcements for his loose-leaf notebook—and we fell into a ridiculous conversation. All of us had a little German, the Japanese had a few snippets of English, about as many as Hightower had of Japanese. Our communication for some reason seemed to us worthy and charming, and we continued it out to the street and into a *Konditorei*, where we became fast friends before we had finished our coffee. After that, for several months, Herr Hai, Hightower, and I met once or twice a week and together we read *Ulysses*, holding the text in three languages. At any rate it *seems* to me we did; I daresay we tried it once and gave up. Somehow the snap went all out of Joyce's puns when we tried them on in German and Japanese. What little German we had, diminished and grew deformed, and we began to forget our own

languages; we remained friends, but I think that
when we met for coffee, we read to ourselves and
simply smiled at one another from time to time.

Mrs. Oswald's conversation with the FBI man
about the diary left me in just about as deep water
as I had been in when I had tried to understand
Hightower's elucidation in German of Joyce's play
on "metempsychosis" to Hai.

"You see, they have never questioned me about
one thing," she went on. "What I'm trying to say
is that the normal thing is they should have been
at my door right away. I *could* have had the diary.
It was my son's diary. But I was never questioned.
So the proof of the pudding is that they knew it
was absolutely leaked, and they let it die down—
you didn't hear any more about it. You see, this is
a good example because *I could have had the diary.*
If they were sincere, they could have come to me,
let's face it. One and one just don't make two. My
book is going to be called *One and One Don't Make
Two* or *This and That.* They're concerned about
the diary, and everybody's investigating, but nobody comes and asks this old mother if she had the
diary and she released it. So I never believed that it
was my son's diary."

I grew increasingly muddled as she escorted me

down cul-de-sacs and through woods which, significantly she felt, could not be seen for the trees. As various as the terrae incognitae were the points of time at which we traversed them. Sometimes I was in New Orleans listening to Lee as he sang "Silent Night" with a "nice little voice," but at the next moment I was at the Six Flags Motel with the Mesdames Marguerite and Marina Oswald after the boy's murder, and johnny-on-the-spot *Life* magazine was there infiltrating the ranks of cops. I examined the contents of Lee's sea bag when he came back from Formosa—he carried with him a book of Christmas carols and a Christmas card from his mother which she had sent him in 1956. I went to Washington with her to the hearings before the Warren Commission and stayed in a suite of rooms the size of a house—dining room, grand piano, everything; I was haunted by the spectral figures of unnamed Secret Service men with a lot of accounting to do, by FBI men who had stayed away from her door, "high officials" who blew their tops when Mrs. Oswald asked them direct questions. I saw a copy of the letter written to Khrushchev (she keeps a copy of everything she writes), I saw a Mother's Day card signed "Lee" that had come from Russia in 1960, and I saw the subpoena requiring her to appear instanter at the Ruby trial. (Sheer perseverance had won her this peremptory invitation: she had been barred from the courtroom.)

The tapes were finally used up and the ashtray beside me was full of cigarette stubs. We stood up and both of us stretched like women who had done a hard day's work cleaning out the cellar and putting up rhubarb. The room was disheveled with exhibits, and the furniture was still out of place where we had moved it to accommodate the tape recorders. I offered to help Mrs. Oswald tidy up, but she said, "No, no, I don't have another thing to do. I was hoping I could give you a bite of supper, but I suppose you can't stay."

"No, I can't," I said. "I'm sorry."

She laughed. "If you cahn't, you cahn't," she said, parodying a broad "a" that does not exist in my speech. "You go on back to Dallas now, and you be fresh for tomorrow because we've still got a lot to talk about, hear? Tomorrow!" She was struck with a numbing thought. "Tomorrow is Mother's Day and I will go to Lee Harvey Oswald's grave, but I will be a mother alone, a mother in history alone on Mother's Day."

A vaporing cloak of wistfulness enveloped her

73

for no longer than the twinkling of an eye. Resourceful woman, she found a dandy solution to her dilemma, and gaily, as if she were planning a picnic or a frisk through an amusement park, she said, "I know! I'll take *you!*"

III

Infernal thunderclaps shocked me awake on Mother's Day, and the rain on my windows sounded like kettledrums being belted by a gang of lunatics. A dolorous gloaming hung in my air-conditioned room, where the temperature was always that of a meat cooler (the windows, of course, could not be opened, so that even on a warm day I had gooseflesh if I took off my sweater), and the rushing wetness outside was a palpable ectoplasm within. My impulse was to eliminate the day by taking a sleeping pill, but I was committed; I must go with Mrs. Oswald to her son's grave.

For a long time I lay abed dawdling over a great pot of coffee and the Dallas *News*. Pitching and tossing through the dispatches from South Vietnam and the Dominican Republic, I had the dislocating feeling that I was not reading about the culmination of crises today that would be annulled by different ones tomorrow, but that I was trying to get into my head the complicated background and causes of a *fait accompli* for a history examination. The living, current, and inexplicable chaos was not happening plangently in South Asia or in the West Indies; it was not political upheaval and war. It was the assassination of President Kennedy that had had taken place only hours—or even minutes—ago.

Probably the storm through which we drove to Fort Worth was not the very worst I had ever seen, but at the time I could not recall another to equal its infuriated lightning and its dooming detonations and the niagaras that roared down on us from four directions, baffling the windshields. It sounded like catastrophe, and I was sorry to be in alien corn. But by the time we got to Mrs. Oswald's street, the fulminations began to peter out and the malevolent splendor was replaced by a sniffling nastiness, the kind of mess that causes angleworms to materialize, mauve and visceral, on sidewalks.

Somewhere in the neighborhood a voice, much amplified, was blaring. I thought at first it was coming from the sound truck of a political candidate on a mobile stump or from one advertising an American Legion carnival, but as I got out of the car, I realized that it was pouring out of Mrs. Oswald's house and that the voice belonged to her. I knocked, unheard, several times. The tulips, I saw, had been decapitated by the wind and their stems were limp among the stiff spears of the everlasting humbug heather.

"What an injustice to a mother!" shouted Mrs. Oswald's disembodied voice. "If this was true, the facts couldn't hurt me so deeply, or I would say, 'Consider the source.' But this quote, along with many others, has gone all over the world and I have been attacked publicly as a mother by television commentators. They said I was going from place to place speaking in behalf of my son. Was it because I wanted to vindicate myself as a mother? What an awful thing! I have taken this with all the composure I know how, but inwardly I have seethed."

The door was open, but the screen was latched. The tape recorders were on the floor, where we had left them yesterday, and I could see the discs of both revolving as they released a hundred and eighty words a minute. I knocked again more loudly and called out. In a moment, Mrs. Oswald appeared. I had interrupted her in the middle of her lunch, and she continued to chew through her welcoming smile as she opened the screen. She was behindhand, she explained, because she thought I might be delayed by the storm—she herself thought nothing of these funny old Texas storms and loved driving through them, but she didn't know how people from Massachusetts took to Wild West weather. (As I have said, I had come down from Connecticut and she had my address there. But this kind of minutia did not concern her. From time to time she had advised me to look something up in the Warren Report, and she would preface this by saying alternately, "When you get back to New York," or "When you get back to Boston." Once, experimentally, I said that I would soon have to return to my post at Austin, and this news had no effect at all.)

I made out her observations about the comical Ole Wild West storms largely by reading her lips, since her recorded voice drowned out her current one. She let me in and turned the volume down and invited me to join her in a snack. I thanked her and refused and asked if I might put my soaked umbrella in the bathroom.

The living room was even more disordered than

it had been when I left it the day before. The coffee table was piled high with newspaper clippings and pamphlets and Xeroxed documents; the lids of the tape recorders lay on the floor, and their canvas covers were wadded up as if someone had meant to throw them out but hadn't got around to it. Evidently Mrs. Oswald had been so busy in my absence that she had let her nest go hang.

The bedroom, however, was as neat as if no one had ever slept or dressed in it, and in the ascetic, antiseptic bathroom, besides the towels imprinted with unlikely anemones, the only things I saw were a bottle of hand lotion named "To a Wild Rose" and an ornamental bar of soap embossed with sharp golden lilies. If Mrs. Oswald suffered from dyspepsia or conjunctivitis, she did not tell the world about it by leaving her medicaments on view.

In the living room, the affirmative voice went on: "I understand that Mr. William Manchester was commissioned by the Kennedy family to rewrite the events of the three days and his book will be out on November 22, 1968. Mr. Manchester is the author of *Profiles in Courage*."

(She had told me this earlier, and when I had diffidently suggested that perhaps she had the title confused with Manchester's book called *Portrait*

of a President, she indicated that the confusion re-
sided in my addlepate. Today she went on record.)

"I would like to say now, unless Mr. William
Manchester discusses my life and my son's life per-
sonally with me, this book will also be inaccurate.
He came to see me, but he was here no more than
ten or fifteen minutes. However, there was one
very important question he asked: and I will tell
you the question. He asked me what a certain party
looked like, and did I have a picture of this certain
party. I didn't ask any questions, and he just stayed
about ten minutes in my home. I say he will make
the same mistakes as the Commission members unless he cooperates with me about my life and my
son's life. This is why there's so many distortions
in the Warren Report. They spoke to outsiders and
they questioned my boys about age six and seven
that couldn't remember things, and they didn't have
the courtesy to come to me and verify these facts.
They printed whatever they were told. And so I
state here and now to the American people that if
Mr. Manchester does not spend at least four days
with me, the Kennedy book will also be inaccurate.
Because I feel like I, Mrs. Marguerite Oswald, is
the only one that can rectify some of the inaccuracies. I am the mother of this boy. The other

two boys were in the service, they don't know about a lot of our life and it has to come from me.

"Many of the readers are wondering, 'Well, why doesn't Mrs. Oswald put all of this into one book so that we can get some of the true story?' It is impossible, dear reader. To begin with, this book would have to be researched for about a year or so. And no one has come to my aid—no publisher with the money, or a writer to do this type work. So until that time and money are afforded me, I will do the best I can. I will admit it is not enough, but as a mother I am doing the best I can."

I looked at myself in the mirror over the washbasin and stuck out my tongue and then went back to the living room. Mrs. Oswald was at her dining table, proceeding with her plentiful lunch. She got up and shut off the machines, and she explained, "I'll start this over from the beginning for you. You see, when I got up this morning, I thought I'd just put something on the tape all on my own. We can erase it if you don't like it, but I really and truly think I have some good instances here for you. I've got some real dynamite and some real exclusives."

I was not pleased, by any means. I had brought no other tapes and there were several questions I wanted to ask her, but erasing all that yardage scared me because I was sure we would botch it and there would be nothing left; so I managed an accepting smile and sat down, prepared to listen.

"Can you do more than one thing at a time?" she asked. "I mean, can you listen and read and so on and so forth, all at once? I can. I can cook and look at TV and clean house and this and that— busy, busy, busy. Some one of the reporters wrote me up as 'The Unsinkable Mrs. Oswald.' Because if you can, I want you to look at these scrapbooks and some other things. I'll just go on and finish my dinner."

In point of fact, I cannot easily assign my attention to two foci simultaneously, and it sets my teeth on edge to hear Scarlatti on a phonograph while cocktail conversation is going on; I can be seduced to attitudes I despise if a symphony is the background to a discussion of zoning laws. But Mrs. Oswald sat me down before a pile of albums and then went to fool with the tape recorders and recited excerpts of her litany to the American way of life, and I had no choice but to divide myself into several receptacles.

There were four big green albums of newspaper clippings, one devoted to Lee, one to Marina, one to Ruby, and one to herself. They were kept meticulously; each clipping adhered to the page in precise relation to the edges, and all were protected by jackets of thick cellophane. Once I was arrested by surprise and a fleeting pity: in the album about herself (the headlines read "Mrs. Oswald Continues Talkathon in Washington," "Mother of Kennedy Assassin Arrives Here to Talk"), I found a small pressed flower, a cluster of trailing arbutus perhaps, or a star of Bethlehem.

Nothing in the memory books was news to me, and so, although I dutifully turned the pages, I was not reading but was listening to Mrs. Oswald's Mother's Day Epistle.

It began serenely: "Upon waking up this morning, and it being Mother's Day, I've decided that in defense of myself and my son, Lee Harvey Oswald, I would put a little something on the tape. I sincerely hope that you will find it newsworthy and print it. Here again, I know you want just a casual interview and you want to keep away from the Warren Commission Report, but because it is involved in my personal life and that of my son, I will have to go back to it from time to time.

"Now they talked about me working as an insurance lady. Here on page 378 of the Warren

Commission Report they say, 'She would sometimes take Lee with her, apparently leaving him alone in the car while she transacted her business. Once she worked during the school year. Lee had to leave an empty house in the morning and return to it for lunch and again at night. His mother having trained him to do that rather than to play with other children.' What an injustice! Anybody who ever sold insurance, and there are many, many insurance men that are going to read this and listen to me and know, a person like I was selling insurance and didn't want to make a killing, we could go out in one hour's time and collect thirty dollars. And so I was home most of the time with my boy Lee. I was usually with him unless I had a definite appointment. I always tried to make my appointments later on, when both the man and the woman were at home, because I found in the beginning when I started to sell and I talked to the woman I was asked to come back to discuss it with the husband. Well, then I would be immediately rejected at the door, and the simple reason for that was that the wife had discussed what I said with the husband, and of course she didn't know as much about it as I did and she didn't present a good case. So I would have definite appointments instead, and usually, out of the four or five calls, I would sell something.

"Now about did he play with other children. When Lee was eleven years old, he visited my sister in New Orleans, Louisiana, which is five hundred and twenty-five miles from Fort Worth. I put him on a train and alone he went. I did caution him to be very careful and not go with strangers or talk with any men who might want to make his acquaintance, and there again I am proud that I thought about these things. This is motherhood. Yet I was criticized in the Warren Report. My sister told the story that I told Lee not to talk to anyone, and it was taken up quite a bit—I think about a page long. That this is what I taught Lee in life, to be by himself. No, no, this is not the case at all. This was a particular instance. And I also told him when he went to school not to go in a car with a stranger, and isn't this what we teach our children? In defense of motherhood also, Lee stayed at my sister's home for two weeks, and that was the arrangement. My sister remarks in her testimony that while he was there he refused to play with any other children. She went into great detail that they tried to get him out of the house and play with the children. Let's understand things a little bit! Here was a perfect stranger, a visitor, he hadn't lived in New Orleans since he was five years old. Now he's eleven and he knew no one in the neighborhood. How do you get an eleven-year-old boy a girl, who in this day and age is almost at maturity? I have to smile because the whole thing is so ridiculous."

I glanced over at the diner, who smiled in confirmation, and I believe I smiled, too.

"Did she bring any eleven- or twelve-year-olds into the home for Lee to meet? And did he refuse to meet them and go off and play with them? Ah! That would be different, but, no, no, she didn't like him in the house listening to television or reading comic books. She wanted him to go out and play with other children. What other children were there for Lee to play with? So again, let's have defense of Lee Harvey Oswald.

"Another thing I objected to in my sister's testimony, when Mr. Jenner asked if any of her boys sold newspapers, and she said, oh, yes, her son Gene did, and she wanted them to know that he saved his money and bought war bonds with it. Well, this is a remarkable and admirable thing for a boy to do. And Mr. Jenner asked if she ever knew that Lee sold papers and she said no, and there was other people questioned about that. There again, I go

in defense of my son. Lee traveled with me and
Mr. Eckdahl, and when he did go to school he was
at an age where he couldn't even be hired to sell
newspapers. The boys in the newspaper business
were fifteen and sixteen years old, which is the
trend today. My own newspaper boy is about seven-
teen years old, and these boys are working their
way through college. Now, we're talking about a
young boy, because this was before age thirteen,
before the New York episode. But you see, I'm
proud of my sister's boys. I think she has a nice family, but let's go a little deeper into an understand-
ing. She remarked very proudly that her boy bought
war bonds. *Her* boy had a father who was in the
bookmaking business and had a very large income—
they own their own home. He was very liberal with
his money, and even though Gene did have a newspaper route, he did not contribute to the household.
As a matter of fact, his father gave him lunch
money besides. So you see this is the difference, let's
face it. This is where the human element comes in.
This is where I have been persecuted. I have shed
many a tear."

My brains were scrambled eggs. I was reminded,
as I tossed in the sponge and gave up trying to
proceed from *a* to *b* to *c*, of one of those games in

which you are meant to direct a blob of mercury, by clever twists of the wrist, through a maze so that it fetches up, all of a piece, in a central zone. Sometimes the blob sprawls out like an amoeba and at other times it multiplies itself by twenty so that there are tiny beads all over the place; sometimes the integer remains but takes a wayward route and lodges far from the goal. Such a plaything (*soi-disant*) can lead to temper tantrums in the middle-aged. I could get no foothold in Mrs. Oswald's reminiscences, and yet, while my mind roved aimlessly every which way, it remained here in this room and on this day. I tried, during the sporadic bursts of thunder and short-lived, violent spates, to transport myself to a ship my husband and I had once taken from the Piraeus to New York in November, when the seas were the kind that had wrecked the *Hesperus;* but I couldn't pay heed to the memory. Usually when I am totally bewildered (this happens to me often at the opera and ninety-two percent of the time when I am listening to a learned paper or a political speech) I can get my bearings by reciting the names of the states or by declining a *stark männlich* noun (I use *der Stuhl*) and then a *schwach weiblich* one (*die Frau*) and a *gemischt sächlich* one (*das Ohr* is as a good a cas-

trato as any); but today I couldn't summon up
more than a score of states, and German declen-
sions were quite out of the question. So I went back
to following the leader on my great leaden clod-
hoppers.

". . . And these are the things I have the abil-
ity of noticing. Why? Because it's affecting me per-
sonally and I'm this type person. Lee was this type
person, he had wisdom. He didn't have—well, he
finished his high school education in the Marines,
and I wouldn't say he was an uneducated man,
knowing Russian like he did and a little Spanish
and German, just a young boy. You know, Russian's a very hard language. But a formal education,
he did not have. He had the know-how. I myself
don't have a high school education and I know I
speak very bad English, but a ten thousand dollar
a year engineering man begged me to marry him.
I made him wait a year, and he was a Harvard
man. I've been on television with the highest caliber
of people and held my own, so I don't think I do
so bad in that department. I'm uneducated, but
very versatile.

"I think it's a natural thing, it isn't anything
that I've studied or learned, it's just doing things
that come naturally, as the phrase goes, and Lee

9 1

had it. Believe me, Lee Harvey Oswald had this natural wisdom. Some people with a formal education are so dull that really and truly I find them stupid. All they know is what's in the books, and that's that.''

I gave up counting on the disclosure of the "exclusives" she had hinted at; the dynamite did not go off.

"I didn't date," I heard her tell dear reader. "My son John said before the commission, 'She didn't have any friends.' Of course I didn't have any friends. Why? Because I was a *mother, a working mother!* When I came home, I had to take care of the house and the groceries and make sure that my children had clean clothes, so what time did I have for friends? I think this is in my favor, that I didn't run around with men and drink and deprive my children. I devoted my life to you boys!''

Throughout the soliloquy, the performer herself sat rapt, her elbows among her lunch dishes. Although her house was temporarily a fright, she was not. She was wearing a trim green linen suit with a smart white blouse. I had the feeling that, except when she was in bed, she was never *en déshabillé*, but was always dressed ready to receive anyone who wished to have the scales removed from his eyes, and that in one of her bureau draw-

ers there was a pile of clean white gloves. It was
evident that she knew and cared about clothes; I
had heard that she occasionally went into Neiman-
Marcus to try on coats and dresses. She was one
of those women whose eye can go directly to the
one appropriate thing on a rack of cheap clothes,
who can shop triumphantly in a bargain basement,
an outlet store, or a thrift shop. This is an urban
gift, but if she had been a country woman, she
could have made unerring selections from a mail-
order catalogue or run up her wardrobe on a sewing
machine with professional results. She would never
make the mistake of going in for conspicuous nov-
elty; if she wore costume jewelry, it would not be
gauche. If she were to travel with those bands of
women that you see in the summer in Europe, her
drip-drys would do what they are advertised to
do and not dissolve or come out irremediably
wadded up.

"And let me tell you this, if you research the
life of Jesus Christ, you find that you never did
hear anything more about the mother of Jesus,
Mary, after He was crucified. And really nobody
has worried about my welfare. Now when I say I
get letters, I mean they are from the public and
they are the only thing that keep me going and I

bless them for it. But I'm talking about my children, my sister. No one, when my son was murdered, no member of the family, no immediate friend came to me and gave me consolation. They didn't want to be involved, you see. You say, 'Your nieces and nephews couldn't send a telegram or a note? Your own sons and their wives?' But I'm gonna be honest with you—not a soul . . ."

The tape ended abruptly; the coda was a metallic squawk.

"How's that?" said Mrs. Oswald, poised, gratified by the ovation she was receiving from beyond the footlights. "Oh, how I wish there was more time! I have stories and coincidences by the galore, and things that I can prove are not according to Hoyle. If we just had the time, we could write them up and become millionairesses. The first book in the series would be *One and One Make Two*."

She had suggested this title in our first interview, and in the second had revised it to *One and One Don't Make Two*. Possibly they were to be in sequel, two volumes, boxed.

As she talked, she unplugged the recorders and removed the tapes, but replacing the covers flummoxed her and she laughed. "Let's get our Yankee

mechanical genius to work," she said, and made a
flirtatious *moue*. "Hurry on, now. I want you to see
the grave by daylight."

I restored the covers and put the canvas overcoats
on the machines while Mrs. Oswald went to get
my umbrella and her purse. She locked the bedroom door after her, and she double-locked the
outer door. "Of course I don't dare keep the really
valuable things in the house. They're in storage,
insured, but even so, there's plenty here that inter-
tested parties could steal, and I can't run the risk."

Her Buick Skylark was blue and new and dapper,
as lovingly tended as Whistler's "Mother." "My
money from *Esquire* paid for this," she said. "I
could have got a lot more for those letters from
Lee if I'd held out, but I felt it was my duty to the
American people to release them when I did."

Her garage was narrow and her uphill driveway
was muddy and the turn at the top was awkward;
she maneuvered the obstacles with skill and aplomb
and drove off through the wet streets as if the car
were a friend whose company she liked better than
any other in the world. I do not drive and I am an
edgy passenger and I sense incompetence immediately, but I felt safe with this able woman: she respected her property and her person too much to

get us into any trouble. I had been wondering from the beginning what she would do with money if a windfall showered her out of the blue, and now I knew at least one place a chunk of it would go, and that would be into the purchase of a high-class automobile with all the fixings. My driver's black limousine was lubberly behind us.

Mrs. Oswald said she would like to stop at the post office because quite often she got a good deal of mail on Sunday. "Oh, the letters I got at the beginning! People writing to ask for my autograph, and of course at that time I was just a novice and didn't know any better and would give it. But now I don't. Hemingway always said, 'All right, you can have my autograph if you pay for it,' and I take the same stand."

I am in luck. I have a note from her and it is signed "Marguerite Oswald, Mother of Lee Harvey Oswald." The "O" is shaped like a heart with a scimitar through it.

She came back from the post office empty-handed, but said that Mother's Day might have something to do with the fact that she had got no letters. "I certainly do want to take the opportunity to thank all the people that write me," she said. "They write me in connection with what I am doing, and they are the ones that give me the courage to continue in what I believe is right. Our American way of life is my theme."

"Yes, I know," I said. "Did you like New York?"

"Oh, I liked New York. I went there because John Edward was there and he was in the Coast Guard at that particular time. He was stationed at Staten Island and never moved around, so he and his wife were kind of staple. Of course I didn't expect to live with my daughter-in-law, but that's where I did go when I first got to New York, until I could find a place and housing—you know there's housing in New York."

I agreed, even though by now I knew that she was not interested in any response of any sort to anything.

"Then through some friends of my daughter-in-law's they found me an apartment and I was delighted. It was five blocks from my son's house, but when I went to pay them the man said, well, you'll have to give a hundred dollars under the table. Coming from Texas and not having housing regulations, I didn't even know what he was talking about. He said, well, apartments were very scarce and in order to get this one you'll have to pay a hundred dollars under the table. Of course I'll never do anything like this. I hurt myself rather than do something like this—it's the principle, let's say. Most people would have thought, I'll just go ahead and pay and be glad to have an apartment, but not me. I think it's just wrong. But then I did get an apartment, and this brings up, did I like New York or didn't I like New York. Yes, I liked New York just fine. I had to leave because of Lee. He couldn't adjust to New York. It was so different—apartment-house living, and such a mixture of different people, and he was a young boy. He was in these segregated schools and they called him a rebel and he was talking about them as a Yankee. I mean, this is a regular trend and nothing abnormal.

"Every Sunday we would go visit the Museum of Natural History or the Planetarium and we'd have dinner at Rockefeller Center, and when I would go to work on Monday, they'd say, 'Well, Oswald, tell us New Yorkers what you found out about New York.' I may go to New York one of these days. I like to travel, just like Lee. He was in the Philippines, he was in Corregidor, he was in Formosa, he was in Japan, so he's been all over besides Russia. That boy was being trained. Let me give you an instance of some of the work I've done on him being trained as an agent. I received this letter from him on November 8, 1961. And on the back of the letter it said, 'Name, Address, Male, Occupation,' and then something I couldn't make out. It looked like a '4' and a '1' and then it had a post-office box, 703 in Washington, D.C. When I received this letter, I wrote asking them to tell me about my son because he was in Russia, and I said that on the back of his letter was this post-office box number. Do you know my letter was not answered or returned to me? Now this is *significant:* that box number has that letter to this day. And do you know who the box number is? Veterans of Foreign Wars, in Washington, D.C.! So this is just a little part of my research of Lee."

The sun was fully out, and on either side of the broad highway, a wavering effluvium rose from the flat fields. Herds of Hereford whitefaces grazed in the pastures between archipelagoes of oil drums; the scene looked like a photograph for a geography book in a chapter on "Principal Industries of the States."

"And here's another thing I just can't swallow. Lee *said* he was a Marxist. He went to Russia with all the publicity, he had a Russian wife, we know all these facts, and he was giving out Fair Play for Cuba literature. I don't know, they say it was, it could have been any kind of literature. Someone said to me, 'Miz Oswald, you're just too easy, how do you know it was Fair Play for Cuba literature?' Well, now since I read the Warren Commission Report, I will admit it probably was Fair Play for literature."

(Her slips of the tongue and elisions, though arresting, did not, I think, have any oblique meaning; they happened, most of them at any rate, simply because she talked so fast.)

"So there's nothing to show he did anything shady. He was on a television program, on WDSU, in New Orleans, and he said he was a Marxist, not a Communist, a Marxist. There was a difference and Marina said there was a difference. I don't know about that. But you do have a higher up and you do have an extrasensory perception, and the truth, I think, always prevails. Tomorrow I will show you a picture that will just show how wrong they were in Washington."

"I won't be here tomorrow," I said.

"Oh, yes, I keep forgetting, you have to go back to Boston."

She stopped for a light, and when it had changed and we sailed on, she said, "I have enough material for at least five books. I could write one just on

Mrs. Paine alone—her testimony is really something to break down. And books, I don't know *how* many books I could write about Lee and the way things happened to him all his life. Now here is a good instance. When we came to Texas from New Orleans, he entered Arlington High School. He entered in the end of September, when school opens, and then he joined the service on October 17th. So approximately he was in school four weeks. Yet there are *three* pictures of my son and one that has him laughing and turning around in the classroom for the yearbook. Now why pick out Lee Harvey Oswald? You'll say, 'Miz Oswald, I don't get the point.' Now the point is how it goes on and on and on and on. Lee Harvey Oswald's picture was taken three times at Arlington High School, out of all the boys there. Why? It doesn't make sense, and since I'm not the only one finding these circumstances, I have to wonder."

I looked out my window, and to the fumy fields I mouthed the words, "Miz Oswald, I don't get the point."

"Now this material of mine, we could run it for two or three years every month in a big national magazine, and after that as a sort of a soap opera on radio or even on TV. And then there'd be the paperbacks and the foreign translations and so on and so forth. Couldn't you take the summer off and come on down and rent the other side of the house so we could write it all up? I mean, I would give of my time and voice and let you see the work I've done and we could split the proceeds."

She had at no time expressed the slightest curiosity about me, and I wondered what she thought I was going to take the summer off *from:* from living in Boston, perhaps. I feel quite sure that if one day I had turned up wearing a beard she would have paid no attention.

For some time I had been aware that a cat was lurking nearby, ready to pounce and get my tongue, and at this invitation he succeeded and took it far away. I could do no more than stammer like a schoolgirl, "I don't know."

"I know a discount house where you could get a hot plate cheap, and you could use my icebox," she said, the practical planner working hand in hand with the dreamer. "There's that back porch, so we could wander back and forth, very informal and relaxed, in our housecoats if the weather got hot. We could set up all my exhibits on what-you-call-'ems—sawhorses is what I mean. And buy a couple of tape recorders, and we'd be in business."

"Mmm."

"I don't care about the money. I say money is only good to its use, but I want history to be straightened out. Of course there is the money too. I gave up my job to come to the rescue and I only have twenty-three hundred dollars to my name. I tell you we could make millions and you could become quite well known."

Now we had reached the gates of the cemetery, and she changed her tack.

In the voice of a tourist guide, she said, "Like everything else in life, this is divided up into classes. There is the section for the rich people, and some very fine people are buried there, and there is the one for the poor people, and then there is the one for the middle class. Lee Harvey Oswald is buried in the middle-class section, as it should be according to his station in life."

The graveyard was deserted; we met no other car and we saw no mourners as we spiraled up between granite lambs and marble cherubim, and Mrs. Oswald plaintively remarked on this. "If it had been a sunny day, you'd have seen the cars lined up clear up to the gates, people coming to see where my son is buried."

Then, in a moment, round a bend, we did see a

car ahead of us at the top of a slight rise. "Now,
there!" she said. "There's somebody after all, even
though it isn't such a nice day, and they're coming to see Lee."

We stopped directly behind a car, which, apple
green where it was not besmirched by mud or
scabbed with rust, could not have been less than
twenty years old; it was long and broad and un-
commonly tall, and its rear window was a high,
narrow oval through which no human eye could
see. It looked as if, when it had been new and
probably black, it had been used as a getaway car.
Its occupants were slogging through the mud across
the road as we opened our doors. They were five
boys in their late teens, all rangy and simianly
long-armed and all wearing dirty dungarees, dirty
T-shirts, dirty sneakers, shaggy, dirty hair.

"They're heading straight for Lee," whispered
Mrs. Oswald. "Now it's that age I want to reach
with my books. The young people. I want to write
it all in a way they will understand and know the
truth of history."

She moved purposefully forward, bowing on
either side to her vassals and her audience, and
halted at a grave at the edge of the road. The vile
boys stepped back and she beamed on them benefi-

cently. They quickly fanned out among other graves higher up the slope, but I was conscious of their eyes on us.

The small granite stone that marks Lee Harvey Oswald's grave bears only his name and the dates of his birth and his death. Surrounding it today were half-drowned yellow pansies. Beside it, resting against a wire bracket, was a pale green cross made of styrofoam, the arms of which were wreathed with artificial freesias. A young weeping willow tree grew at the head of the grave, its vulnerable leaves touched quietly by the light, damp breeze. Plastic philodrendron, as glossy as a grass snake, wound up its trunk.

Mrs. Oswald plucked a weed from among the pansies, bent the pliable freesias into a more becoming embrace around the cross, brushed off her hands, and gave me one of them to shake. Her mission was efficiently completed.

"It turned out to be a right nice Mother's Day after all," she said. "But on some Mother's Day, I think it would be wonderful for the United States to come out and say my son was an agent. It would be wonderful if they would come out in behalf of his family and his mother and say he died in the service of his country. They're not all-powerful, and not everything they do is right. I love my United States, but I don't think just because I was born in it, that we're perfect. And I feel that my son Lee Harvey Oswald felt the same way. If he learned those truths from me, I didn't teach him, but if he sensed that was the way I felt, I make no apology for that either. We are not always right and I feel sure that as Americans we know this and we will admit it some day. Let's have a little defense of Lee Harvey Oswald! On Mother's Day, let's come out and say that he died in the service of his country."

"Is that what you mean by your statement on the little scroll?" I asked.

"No comment," said Mrs. Oswald. "I do not comment on my statement." She was curtly official, putting the multiplied me (I was a rude mob of impertinent reporters) in my place; but immediately she was friendly again, perhaps thinking of me as her future collaborator lounging around at ease in my housecoat.

"Now you think about what I said about coming on down here for the summer. I'll be happy to cooperate with you. It would be a big deal."

She dismissed her troops and got into her car, waved absent-mindedly and drove off. As soon as she was gone, the five sightseers converged upon the grave, and my driver, as he opened the door for me, said, "I don't like the looka them. They had a guard on the grave up until a while back. I reckon they figure nobody cares about it no more."

We were silent for several miles, and then he said, "The day it happened I was hauling some folks from Love. Prettiest day you ever did see, and all of a sudden we heard it on the radio that the President was dead. I took this party to their hotel and then I went out in the country and set by myself. I never reported back to work till next morning."

Today as we drove over the road where the motorcade had been hideously halted, bringing the whole world abruptly to a stop, and past the Book Depository whence the bullets had been fired, I observed, as I had done on each of my trips to and from Fort Worth by this same route, that the physical site did not accentuate my recollected woe. Indeed, I was instead returned to my own apartment in New York, where, quite by accident, I had turned on the radio and had heard the first inconclusive bulletins. At other times in my life I have stood on memorable ground and have directly apprehended experience that heretofore had been

once removed because I had only read about it:
once when I drove inland from the Normandy
beaches, I knew for the first time with uncluttered
pain what the invasion had been, and the deaths,
along those pretty lanes and within those pretty
groves of trees, of my frinds and kinsmen became
more than abstractions.

But John Kennedy died everywhere, not more
in Dallas than in Paris or Calcutta or in my apartment in New York City.

Epilogue

I left Dallas the next day in a preposterous storm, five times as rip-roaring as the one the day before. Even for Baron von Munchausen it was laid on too thick. The rain, much wetter than any other I had ever been soaked by, came down hell bent for election, and the lightning was a stretch on the imagination. My plane was two hours late getting in from El Paso and then for another hour, after it did get in, it sat on the field unopened. One of the men at the gate told me, "They can't open the doors. If they did, those passengers would get blown right back to the border." He laughed as he said it, with regional pride.

We were finally allowed to board, escorted by men in nor'westers and hip boots, carrying bumbershoots the size of umbrella trees. One of these turned inside out and the poor fellow who had been handling it was almost lifted off his feet; I would not have been surprised if he'd been swept aloft and had vanished from view, as Sinbad was carried away from the valley of diamonds by the Roc. I thought of a joke one of my drivers had told me. A Texan, visiting Niagara Falls, was asked if there was anything like that in the Lone Start State and he replied, "No, but we've got a plumber in Houston that can fix it." Just about anything can happen in Texas; while I was in Dallas, I heard of a curriculum for pre-pre-school children that included a course in "Remedial Creeping and Crawling."

Once we were off the ground, the commotion died down, and as Texas receded, the firmament grew pure. My flight to New York was as smooth as sleep. But no matter how gentle an airplane ride is, no matter how consolingly cloudless the empyrean, no matter how reassuring the look of the crew, when I am in the sky I meditate on life and death. And now in minute particular I relived the day in 1963 when the random element in the universe went hogwild. Within half an hour of the final awful bulletin from Parkland Memorial Hospital, New York City was as still as a ghost town. The streets were all but deserted; traffic was nearly at a standstill. I tried without success to telephone my husband at *The New Yorker* office—all the telephone lines were jammed, as sometimes they are in a great blizzard.

My husband was ill and had been for a long time and his illness had generated a deep depression. But in the last couple of weeks, he had been sanguine and nearly himself again and we had resumed the life we'd lived before, of having friends in to dinner or going out to his favorite restaurants. The night before, we had made a pub crawl to our familiar saloons, to Bleeck's and P. J. Moriarity's and Tim Costello's and we'd had a good time; tonight, Friday, we planned to go to a fight at the Garden. I can't remember who was fighting that night but it seems to me it may have been Dick Tiger; in any case it was someone Joe thought had talent. Everything, of course, was cancelled. I recall being shocked, I really don't know why, when I heard that some people went ahead and had the dinner parties they'd planned.

It was late in the afternoon when Joe got through to me, and his voice was more despairing than it had been at any other time since he'd been sick. I think I had counted on him to tell me that the news I'd heard on the radio wasn't true, that it was some monstrous hoax, and that a whole world of possibilities still lay open to Kennedy. None of us could believe it. I slept very poorly that night, waking often to the knowledge that something dreadful had happened, and not being able at first to remember what it was, and then remembering. Twice during the night I went in to Joe's room, where he was sleeping lightly too, but he could not tell me that I had only been having a nightmare of stupendous violation.

For days we all went about our business like somnambulists.

After Joe died, a few weeks later, as I was clearing out his office I got rid of pounds and pounds of newspapers that he was using in writing his "Wayward Press" piece, and the headlines freshly flabbergasted me and my rage came back. Suddenly death was larger than life and suddenly it was terrifyingly twice as natural.

Appendices

I

Mrs. Oswald claims that the famous picture of Lee Harvey
with his guns was fabricated, and she said, "Well, actually,
my son has never been indicted for the murder of President
Kennedy, Officer Tippit, or the shots at General Walker.
This is their evaluation. Now I expect to evaluate their
findings a little differently as prior testimony I have been
showing the inaccuracies. But since this is the twentieth
century, I would hope that pictures would do it. I have
many pictures in my possession which prove that things
are not according to Hoyle. And the main picture I have
is a picture of my son, Lee Harvey Oswald, exploited in
the February issue of *Life* magazine, 1963, as the assassin and killer of Tippit, and the gun. This picture is a
fake. I have many, many articles, many books saying it's
a fake. It was told that it was a fake before the Warren
Commission and they go into great detail about this picture
and finally come up with the conclusion that the magazines
and newspapers that had this particular photograph ad-
mitted that they inadvertently removed some of the parts
of the gun from the picture. Now we have three or four
pages on this and it's very official, and it looks like it's
really the truth. I'm sure they were honest about it and
they believe it. I'm going to ask one question and answer
it myself. Mrs. Oswald, what gives you the authority, just
a laywoman, to contradict the Warren Report findings
where they had experts testing the negatives and the
photographs? Well, I went about it in just a little different
way.

"The exact date in April that this photograph was supposed to have been made at 214 Neeley Street, down in West Texas, and taken by my daughter-in-law, Marina Oswald. I took a picture with the same camera. I have proved in 1964 that this picture cannot be taken because of the foliage. I went back in December, 1964, and I took the yard again, which showed the same background of the picture in *Life* magazine. Now in 1965, April, just a few weeks ago, I went back to 214 Neeley Street, and I took photographs again. I'm in the picture each time. You can see only my face because of the foliage, which has to prove that this picture was taken right before the assassination as a plant or immediately after, which would be in the month of November, when this foliage wouldn't be like it would be in April. Now I have these pictures and I would like someone to call my hand on this, some official. Let's get that ball a-rolling."

She showed me the photographs of herself amid shrubbery beside a house, but because my recollection of the background in the photograph of Lee was shadowy, I could not be amazed except at the ingenuity and perseverance of her research.

The day before, in her excoriation of Mrs. Paine, she had said, "And one thing that insults my intelligence, the morning after when we had left, Marina and I had left with the *Life* representative at ten thirty that morning, it says that the police came back to the house later on, so she went to the grocery store and told them to go ahead and search the house. Now I don't know, I just don't swallow some of these things, particularly when they go on and on and on. I don't say it isn't possible that a woman would give the police, invite 'em in, and say, 'You go in the house, I'm going to the grocery store.'

"Well, this was the time they found the pictures! This was the time the police found the pictures that were in the garage, when Mrs. Paine wasn't home and *she* didn't know anything about the pictures. It's proved in the War-ren Commission Report that the Dallas police called that night and asked Mr. Paine to come to the station to identify the *pictures!* And told them that they found the *pictures* in his garage. Well, there's much, much more to this, but this will just give you an idea of the many lies."

Her voice was at its most impassioned and her face at its pinkest with indignation when she talked of the pictures, but the enigma is beyond my elucidation.

II

John Edward Pic, in fact, lived on 92nd Street between First and Second Avenues. Bear in mind that he was stationed on Staten Island, a distance of nearly fifteen miles. Mrs. Oswald had an apartment in the Bronx, but one of the jobs she had took her daily to 42nd Street in Manhattan, and at another time she worked at Martin's department store in the downtown section of Brooklyn, so that she must have traveled almost an hour by subway, surely the least agreeable means of transportation in the world. Why did she not get a job nearer her apartment or an apartment nearer her job?

When she released her son's letters from Russia, she said in her explanatory notes that the reason Lee Harvey had written to her at so many different addresses was that she was a practical nurse and moved from place to place as her services were required. But she was not always a practical nurse, and the Warren Report, as I have indicated, shows that in both New Orleans and Fort Worth she moved continually. Since the assassination, she has had at least three different addresses.

III

One day after I had been to Dallas I was lunching in New York with a psychoanalyst friend of mine and mentioned Mrs. Oswald's saying that Freud had said that if there were no persecution there would be no persecution complex. He told me that Freud had, indeed, written something in the essay *Certain Neurotic Mechanisms in Jealousy, Paranoia and Homosexuality* that could be so construed through either, on the one hand, a superficial reading or, on the other, a very attentive one. I have looked at the essay, but I am altogether out of my depth and leave the interpretation to the doctors. What interests me and what interested my friend is how Mrs. Oswald came by this esoterism.

IV

According to a story that appeared in the New York newspapers, a gun collector named John King claimed that he paid Oswald's widow $10,000 for the Italian army rifle that killed the President and the .38 that killed Officer Tippit, and he was suing the government for them. They had been in Washington, together with all the other evidence accumulated by the Warren Commission, but had then been returned to Dallas, where they were in the custody of the FBI. The Justice Department, in its quite understandable effort to keep the weapons, was being assisted, curiously enough, by the Internal Revenue Service, whose argument was that Oswald falsified papers in buying the guns and they might thereby be confiscated under the Alcohol and Tobacco Tax Unit. The technicality applies to items for which less than $2,500 was paid, and while King said that he paid $10,000, Oswald is said to have bought the rifle and sniperscope for $19.95 and the pistol for $29.95.

On November 2, 1965, President Johnson signed a bill authorizing the federal government to take ownership of the rifle that killed President Kennedy. The new legislation authorizes the attorney general to designate as federal property items of evidence collected by the Warren Commission.